Praise for *Vessel*

"*Vessel* is a powerful current of words, an unmooring exploration of mortality. In its flow it carries lost bodies, fragments of conversation, snippets of philosophy and history. I am grateful for this singular book, its hunger and eloquence."

—Martha Baillie, author of *There Is No Blue*

"Beautiful, and terribly moving. She approaches unbearable loss with a delicate step, and walks right to its core, paying it the deepest possible respect."

—Helen Garner, author of *This House of Grief* and *Monkey Grip*

"*Vessel* interleaves a delicate curation of memory's traces and fragments with poetries of forgetting and remembering. Netherclift is a writer of exceptional lyrical gifts and a brilliant anatomist of memory, even when facing loss and trauma. *Vessel* weighs what might be held in language with what is fleeting and porous in restive, inventive and deeply moving ways."

—Felicity Plunkett, author of *A Kinder Sea* and *Vanishing Point*

"Utterly captivating and written with searing intelligence, Dani Netherclift's *Vessel* is a poetic, tender and moving meditation on grief, time, memory and love and the shapes we leave behind."

—Arlane Beeston, author of *Because I'm Not Myself, You See*

"In a world increasingly indifferent to—or suspicious of—literature, I am supremely grateful for works like *Vessel*: short, intense, deeply intelligent, and profoundly moving. Dani Netherclift's account of loss, and the long process of engaging with that loss, is always compelling. Netherclift has crafted an 'elegiac lyric essay' that is both in touch with its antecedents and unlike anything I have ever read."

—David McCooey, author of *The Book of Falling*

"*Vessel* transcends personal elegy, and becomes something more ambitious: writing as testament; as reclamation; as communion."

—Adele Dumont, for the *Mascara Literary Review*

VESSEL

VESSEL

The Shape of Absent Bodies

Dani Netherclift

Assembly Press
PRINCE EDWARD COUNTY, ONTARIO

First published in Australia by Upswell Publishing, 2024

Library and Archives Canada Cataloguing in Publication
Title: Vessel : the shape of absent bodies / Dani Netherclift.
Names: Netherclift, Dani, author.
Description: Previously published: Perth, Western Australia: Upswell Publishing, 2024.
Identifiers: Canadiana (print) 20250285096 | Canadiana (ebook) 20250286475 | ISBN 9781998336258 (softcover) | ISBN 9781998336265 (EPUB)
Subjects: LCSH: Netherclift, Dani. | LCSH: Netherclift, Dani—Family. | LCSH: Families—Australia—Victoria. | LCSH: Drowning victims—Australia—Victoria. | LCSH: Fathers—Death. | LCSH: Brothers—Death. | LCSH: Grief. | LCGFT: Autobiographies.
Classification: LCC BF575.G7 N475 2026 | DDC 155.9/37—dc23

Published by Assembly Press | assemblypress.ca
Cover design by Greg Tabor

Printed and bound in Canada on uncoated paper made from 100% recycled content in line with our commitment to ethical business practices and sustainability.

Thus untethered, the body no longer possessed situation in the world, and there was nothing more to say about it.

—Sarah Manguso, *The Guardians*

I want you to find me. I want my disappearance to be untranslatable.

—Felicity Plunkett, "Becoming the Sea"

RUSHWORTH - VICTORIA
30OC17

I have a collection of one-hundred-year-old envelopes addressed to my great-grandmother, sent from the trenches in France and Belgium in World War I. The address the envelopes were sent to is the place my father and brother departed from on the day they died. This land, Ngurai-illum Wurrung Country, forty acres, shaped like a lopsided house turned on its side, was colonised by my Scottish ancestors one hundred and seventy years ago.

These envelopes are empty now.

It is the second day of the year.

1993. A Saturday. Thirty-eight degrees Celsius. I don't know what time it is when I witness my father and brother drown, minutes—perhaps only seconds—apart. Maybe the times of their deaths are listed somewhere in the coroner's reports, but if they are, they can be only estimates. If I had to guess, I would say they died sometime between three and four o'clock in the afternoon when the sun hung high in the sky, garlanded by cumulus clouds with plans in the wings. How long did it take? There is an answer, but nobody knows it. This time, and the time following their disappearance from sight, is lost time, or time turned outside itself. It has no shape, no meaning.

What is the ticking of a clock to the submersion of breath?

My father drives his yellow ute the distance from this ancestor land, Ngurai-illum Wurrung Country, to the channel. In the front with him, my cousin. In the back, in the sun and wind, I sit with my brother and the dog, a black Labrador. The drive takes minutes, is walking distance. My boyfriend N— and I walk this way the following day, over dirt road and native-grass verge, but the road has changed by then.

The site of their deaths is a man-made place, a tributary or irrigation channel deriving from the Waranga Basin in North East Victoria. Years later, for the purposes of a civil court case taken against what was then called the Rural Water Corporation, I referred to my police witness statement to verify a detail vividly recalled by both me and my cousin, the other witness to the drownings. The lawyers for the Rural Water Corporation's insurers argued that their client was not responsible for the safety of members of the public in instances where they were recreationally swimming.

I might have a vague memory of a small warning sign. Maybe it said *No Swimming,* or *Swimming is Prohibited,* or *Danger!* The kind of sign no one would have taken literally in my childhood. Though I had never been to this swimming place before, my father had been there every day of that week. On the morning of the drownings, a large amount of water was released into the irrigation channel. Changing the nature of the current, the outcome

of the day,
of our lives.

In the channel there is a flow regulator, or spillway, which creates a brief drop in the water level and a resultant modest waterfall effect. On this day the area beneath this fall is churning, writhing, turning in on itself. It is white water, amber-hearted.

My father strips down to his underwear and walks to a small platform upstream where the channel is one smooth, swiftly flowing brown sheet above the fall. He dives in like a man with no premonition he is about to die.

The dog leaps joyfully into the white water beside where I sit on a patch of concrete next to the spillway. My legs are immersed in falling water, but only as far as my knees. I call to my brother, *The dog's in the water*! His response is to enter the channel immediately beneath the spill, not to swim but to rescue the dog who as it transpires, is least in need of salvation.

In my police statement, recorded about two weeks later, these images of entry are absent. There are descriptions corresponding to this recollection in my cousin's witness statement, but in my version, these small actions go unrecorded. My story, then, is incomplete. Imperfectly told. Punctured with gaps. Imagine white spaces in which the words have been submerged. They're there, but you can't see them below the surface, held beneath that border.

In my memory of my first, informal police statement, given in my grandparents' lounge room sometime late in the afternoon of the day of "the accident," as my family come to call it, it is as if I am watching my own body as though looking down from somewhere else in the room. I see the red-velvet lounge suite. I see myself wedged deep and small into my grandmother's chair, as though trying to make myself disappear (escape all of this), my grandmother's cotton button-up nightie pulled over my small black bikini. Time is arrested. I recall nothing of what I said.

I am first to the water's edge.

I have already stripped down to my bikini in the back of the ute, but when I see the water, when I hear it, I stop short of diving in. I sit down on the rough slab of concrete adjacent to the spill, sticking my feet into the hard gush of brown water. I wait for the others, my father, my big brother, my cousin, to decree its safety. I remain resolutely grounded.

I am eighteen years old.

I have returned the day before to Melbourne after a beach holiday with friends.

There are traces of sand in my hair, in my ears.

This is the girl I was.

The opening of the game season at Rushworth was marred by a sad drowning accident, which occurred about midday, at the Waranga Basin.. The victim was Mr. John Ayres, about 50 years of age. Having shot a duck, he waded in after it. He secured the duck, and was turning round to come out again when he threw up his hands and sank. His son, a lad about 13 years of age, was with him at the time, and conveyed information into the town. Deceased leaves a family of eight children, the youngest but an infant.

Some of the newspapers report that I am fourteen years old. When I give my statement fourteen days afterwards, the policeman who had arrived at the scene of the accident tells me he had assumed my age from the slightness of my body and had wrongly reported it to journalists. He apologises. When this policeman had arrived at the channel, I had asked him to get in touch with my uncle, the father of the cousin with me. I had asked him if he knew my uncle. The policeman was my uncle's next-door-neighbour.

In December 1992, the month before the accident, my brother's dog Bucket went missing at Dights Falls in Melbourne. No trace of the dog was found, though my brother advertised in local papers, offering a $500 reward. There were phone calls, of course, but none were genuine. He still had ads in papers and posters up around town when he died. This detail always feels like a vital clue as to why things happened as they did.

In Sarah Manguso's *The Guardians*, Manguso writes about her friend, Harris, who ended his life by jumping in front of a New York train. Harris had absconded from the psychiatric hospital where he had been admitted during a psychotic episode. The last hours of Harris's life are unaccounted for. Unknowable. Manguso writes that these hours seem missing, but in fact they are only unknown. The interlude before the ending is impossible to divine or at least unfathomable.

Like the last [underwater] moments

of my father's life.
Of my brother's.

When I was growing up, my mother seemed fixated on the obituary columns of newspapers. She scanned them daily. In 1992, the week before my eighteenth birthday, she told my siblings and me of the existence of a hitherto-unknown half-brother. It transpired that my mother had had a baby before the rest of us. Aged sixteen, and herself motherless, she was forced to hide her pregnancy until she was taken to St Joseph's Foundling Home in Broadmeadows to have the child and give him up for adoption. None of us had known that she had been searching for the body of a child.

My great-grandmother, Colina—the receiver of these envelopes and the letters inside them—used to tell the story of her first cousin, Charles, who drowned in the Waranga Basin on his sixteenth birthday in 1908 trying to retrieve a hat. His grave is located perhaps twenty paces away down the quartz hill in the cemetery from my father's and brother's bones.

In the first year of my undergraduate writing degree, I wrote a short story re-imagining Charles's death. It was called "The drowned land." Months later I reread the story after it was published in a literary journal and was bemused to belatedly recognise details of my own experiences of (witnessing) drowning. Or rather, that fragments had rooted themselves unintentionally into the story, like the rictus of a smile in the form of a set of lost false teeth embedded into the soft mud bed of the newly constructed Basin. My father wore false teeth; I don't know if they were still in his mouth when his body was found.

I also created a scene in which the dead boy's grandfather was the one who pulled him from the water and clasped his body tenderly all the way back to shore. In my story, the boy's corpse was just a no-longer-living version of a boy. I don't mean to suggest I wrote these things blindly, that I don't recall constructing the details. It's just that at the time I thought I was only writing a story about a boy who died a long time ago. I didn't dredge up details from my own experience, not consciously.

On Tuesday, three days and nights after he has drowned, my brother's body is found.

My grandfather is informed by the police beforehand of the presence of *something* in the net hanging off the bridge downstream. He tells the rest of us, who are waiting, hoping for this news. We are too shocked for grief, in disbelief still, an in-between-place. My grandfather insists on being present at the channel, sitting in his car as the body of my brother is pulled up in the net like a haul of fish.

My grandfather is there, but he keeps his eyes downcast. My brother, his body, is only witnessed in a blur of peripheral shape.

I want to say I remember everything; that, in seeing, I took it all in. But at the time, even seeing all that, my brain baulked at any comprehension of *drowning*, at a joining of the witnessing and the word. I viewed my father and brother through the lens of being *in trouble*, struggling, in danger, but there was no seed of the possibility of death, that *that's* what we were witnessing. Not even after they were submerged. It took a long time for that knowledge to settle.

I don't know about the parts of what I saw that never even made it into my consciousness.

Details I might never recall, much as

I
want
to
say,

I remember everything.

In the prologue to Michael Cunningham's 1999 novel *The Hours*, he describes an omniscient view of Virginia Woolf's drowning. His words elucidate Woolf's act of entering the river near her house, her coat pockets filled with smooth river stones. The prose travels along with Woolf's body, long after she has perished, following its journey to a destination beneath a bridge far downriver. In Cunningham's version, the body at this final point encounters from a distance the actions of a small boy and his mother standing on the bridge above and assimilates them into the heart of its matter.

The word "deceased" comes from decease + ed, from Middle English, *deceas* via old French, from Latin *dēcessus* (to depart), equivalent to dēced–, variation of *dēcēdō, dēcēdēre* (to go away).

The report detailing the coroner's findings states that my brother's body was found *wedged* beneath a pylon under a bridge downstream from where I last saw him. I don't recall any findings besides this one image.

I return to the scene of the accident two or three times during the week following the deaths. The first time the next day, with my boyfriend N—. I try to describe to N— what happened and how, but the heavy flow of water has been turned off the night before to assist in the search for the bodies, so the place where they died doesn't exist in the same way it did the day before. My brother's body is still in the water. We didn't know how close he was, then. That opaque material.

In newspaper photographs in the local paper that week, I see two men standing near to where my father dived in. The men are staring out across the channel in the search for the bodies. In another photo, there is no water at all flowing over the spillway. You can see the concrete and steel bones of the flow regulator, its inner workings.

I visit the spillway another time, with a small group of family and friends, before my brother's body is recovered. They try to make connections between the now-sluggish water and what has occurred. It makes no sense to them. We see the net hanging from the bridge, waiting for its catch. We have gathered an enormous bunch of yellow everlasting daisies from the bush. We leave the flowers on the bank; I refuse to give anything to the water. I see it as somehow embodied, monstrous. It's mere coincidence the flowers are left at the site of my witnessing, next to the slab of concrete where I stood as my father and brother entered the channel.

I go back once more to the channel after my eldest brother J— returns from his overseas honeymoon a couple of weeks later and is met with news of the drownings. I try once again to describe the accident in a way that might make it coherent, but my words are inadequate to the task. Again, the water has lost the rushing madness of the day of the accident. It seems meek now, benign. Not that people don't drown in water like that. People drown in bathtubs.

A few years ago, returning to the spillway for the first time in decades, I noticed a brass plaque affixed to the concrete bridge downstream. It commemorates a dead fisherman. The plaque is attached to the part of the bridge where the net that caught my brother hung years earlier.

When I think of the net, my mind confuses it with the rope we threw towards my father and brother. In my mind's eye, the net is made of the same material.

On the night of the accident, I comfort my sister, brushing her hair with the pink hairbrush our grandmother has earlier used to brush mine. My sister does not realise our father's and brother's bodies have not been recovered. She has only been told they have drowned. This comes to light when a late-night phone call from the police informs the gathered family that our father, his body, has been found by divers. The search is being wound down for the night. Regarding the body of our brother, I soothe my sister with words—

It's not him anymore. He's not there.

But he is still there, or the shape of him is.

The shape of what he has been, up until now.

Though I have witnessed every moment of the drownings, after the accident—when nobody else knows yet—when my grandfather begins to make phone calls, I hear him speaking words I haven't considered up until now, words I have refused entry to—*Dead. Died. Drowned. [Double] tragedy*—it doesn't seem real. I don't want to believe the words. I start moaning quietly, a hum, a keening, because now it has been put into words, these words, a lexicon of endings, I know it is true. The knowledge sets on my skin like a carapace, a papier-mâché casing layering itself over and over the girl I've been until now.

I say—*Though I witnessed every moment of their drownings,*

but I didn't witness every moment, only the parts I could see.

I say—*I saw them die,*

but I'm sure their hearts were still beating the last time I saw them.

I say—*I'm sure.*

WARANGA BASIN WATERS.

MELBOURNE, Monday.

The Deputy Chief Engineer of Water Supply (Mr. Dethridge) confirmed the statement made by an officer of that department that the water which was flowing into the Waranga Basin from the Rushworth mine, in which the bodies of the man and woman were lately found, would not pollute the water of the basin.

Mr Dethridge remarked that if the bodies were found in the reservoir itself it would not be practicable to pump the reservoir dry. Mr Dethridge added that the present depth of the reservoir was 16 feet, and it had a surface area of 16 square miles, and a volume of 6,000 million cubic feet. What the department was more concerned about than the pollution of a small amount of water by the fact of the presence of two human bodies, Mr Dethridge continued, was the inflow of the mineral water, but the amount that any ordinary mining machinery could pump would not have any appreciable effect on such a large volume of water.

Mr Dethridge said, in answer to a question, that some years ago a man had been drowned in the Malmsbury reservoir, but the body was found in two or three days.

Though it occurred within what I refer to as time outside of time, the archive states that my father's body is found at *about 10:30 p.m.* As to the concreteness of location, of distances, of directions, his body is located *Approximately 100 metres west of where he had entered the channel.*

The Waranga-Western-Mallee Channel is a man-made body stemming from the Waranga Basin. The irrigation channels were designed to carry water to parched western plains. This channel begins in the locality that my father was born in, Ngurai-illum Wurrung Country, in the Kulin Nation—North East Victoria, and ends at the beginning of the Mallee region, Dja Dja Wurrung Country. When I was a child, my family lived at the other end of the channel. As children, we swam those waters. As a child, my father had swum them. They were joyful waters to us, who were people born far from the salt waters that bore our ancestors to these shores.

The night of the accident, I try to sleep, but each time I close my eyes the scenes from the channel replay behind my eyelids. I am terrified. I can't bear to be alone. A vision manifests, of cumulus clouds floating serenely down from the sky to the mess of water beneath the spillway. The clouds scoop my father and brother up, enclosing them, removing them from chaos, delivering them into sky. In this vision, the bodies of my father and brother are sleeping forms, at peace, and I am finally lulled to sleep.

I have a postcard, a print of a Marc Chagall painting, *The Creation of Man,* that my friend H— sent me from France in the late 1990s. The colourful detail at the top of the painting depicts religious scenes, a (the?) crucifixion, crowds of people. The naked body of a man is cradled gently by an ascending angel, but what I notice most is the blue outline of what appears to be a cloud enclosing the entire scene. At the bottom of the painting, also enclosed in blue, stand a man, a girl, and what might be a dog.

The day I first met H— we were both fifteen years old; she had received news only the day before that her older brother had died in a jump from a bridge in Queensland. Much later, when we had become close friends, she told me every bone in her brother's body had been broken in the fall.

When I wake with the dawn light the morning after the accident, realisation breaks the peace of sleep. The household is still, sleeping after the long night. I wander around outside and stumble upon the sight of my grandfather sitting in the driver's seat of his old brown Holden ute at the threshold of a partial bush paddock. My grandfather's feet are planted on the ground, his face cradled by, and covered with, his large hands. He does not see me, seeing him.

Fourteen years later, I enter through this gateway dressed in white, and marry my husband in the yellowed paddock beyond.

I have had the florist make extra buttonholes of white rose and glossy camellia leaves. In the morning, after I have my makeup and hair done, but before I put on my wedding dress, I go to the nearby cemetery and lay the buttonholes on the graves of my father and brother. In my absence, the photographer arrives. She expresses distaste for the idea of my visiting graves on my wedding day and chastises me when I return.

It's easy to forget how desperate we were to find my brother's body. After the police divers left, we plotted ways to take matters into our own hands. My uncle wanted to don his wetsuit, enter the opaque water himself. Meanwhile, my aunty sent a letter to the local member to ask what was being done to find the body of my brother. Why he (?) had been left drifting so long.

It's easy to forget we were praying to and bargaining with a god we'd paid scant attention to before. We rationalised scenarios in which my brother's (living) body had made it somehow far downstream. That he had been washed up alive, was wandering, confused,

maybe amnesiac,
that he had survived—
was only lost, as in misplaced.

In June 2022, Anita Alvarez, an American artistic swimmer in the World Aquatic Championship in Budapest, performed her routine before fainting in the water. Her body's graceful descent to the bottom of the deep clear pool was recorded and broadcast in video stills. A body will sink this way because the lungs have filled with water. Moments later, Alvarez's coach, a former Olympian athlete, dived into the pool fully clothed and pulled Alvarez to the surface where she was resuscitated. She recovered completely. Each time I saw this image of rescue, the two women at the bottom of the pool, I began to cry. It was something about the inert form of the unconscious swimmer combined with the complete clarity, the stillness of the water. It seemed a kind of miracle that under these circumstances a swimmer did not simply disappear beneath a surface, was not lost forever, but could be saved. Everything—life, death—depending upon mere clarity. Upon stillness.

In 2015, famed Russian free diver Natalia Molchanova vanished in the Balearic Sea off the eastern coast of Spain. Molchanova—who held the world record for holding her breath underwater, for a fraction over nine minutes—was teaching inexperienced divers, but on one solo dive, she didn't emerge from the water. Her body was never found.

Luc Besson's French film *Le Grand Bleu*—better known to English speaking audiences as *The Big Blue*— portrays a fictionalised and dramatized account of the friendship and rivalry between free divers Jacques Mayol and Enzo Maiorca. In the film, Enzo perishes on a free dive to four hundred metres, due to the effects of deep-water pressure. Later, Jacques dives to the same, biologically untenable depth. The ending of the film has two versions—in the original French conclusion, Jacque's fate is left deliberately ambiguous, to illustrate the possibility both of death, and of a state of true affinity with the "big blue" of the sea—but in the US version, an additional scene shows Jacques implausibly returning to the surface.

My second cousin, M—, died aged twelve in a country pool in the 1980s during a school swimming lesson. He went into cardiac arrest and was found at the bottom of those clear waters. As a child, this image of him floating in such transparent waters, so alone, unsaved/unseen, haunted me. Only very recently did I realise I had transposed onto this drowning the image of the swimming pools I had swum in as a child. The pool that M— drowned in is a cordoned-off rectangle at the shore of Lake Mulwala. The lake is far from transparent. It is the same colour as the waters of the irrigation channel.

An immersed body almost always assumes a face-down position due to the relative weight of limbs in comparison to the trunk. Alvarez's body, as drowning woman at the bottom of the pool, is face down.

Perhaps my father's and brother's bodies would have formed similar shapes?

There is something tremendously moving in the way of beautiful things [Ophelia-like] in the image of Alvarez's still body in clear water at the bottom of the pool.

This is the way I imagine my brother's lost body during the days and nights he is missing. *Not him anymore*. Yet still him, the shape of him

as in slumber

or simply

as an emptied vessel
obscured by water.

Not as a body subjected to the violence of nature's afterword. No, untouched. Intact. Still Him.

In the state of Idaho in the USA, Sandy and Gene Ralston, a married couple of biologists in their seventies, have devoted their retirement years to searching for often-long-lost bodies in water. They do so at their own expense with their own equipment, using a technique called side-scan sonar. They have identified the resting places of more than one hundred and twenty bodies, which have then been retrieved by authorities. The oldest body they have found had been missing for twenty-nine years (the number of years, at the time of writing, since my father and brother drowned).

One woman, whose father's body had been missing for fifteen years, contacted the Ralstons to help find him. The daughter had been eighteen years old when her father disappeared in an immense reservoir in Wyoming. The Ralstons located the body in eight minutes. When the body of the man was brought up a month later by authorities, his wife and son and daughter were waiting. The daughter said that the water had been very cold, and the body had been relatively well preserved. All three of them lavished embraces and kisses upon this drowned body. The father's body was still recognisably *him. His shoulder felt like a shoulder, and it was very, very surreal to be able to hug him again. It was the most happy, saddest day of my life. We got to find him, then I had to say goodbye again.*[1]

The body of a drowned man is not a poem,
and yet his body can be transformed into words,
so that it is letters that are sloughed off (not skin).
The chromatic and achromatic nature of
bodies
rendered otherwise,
a matter of editing.

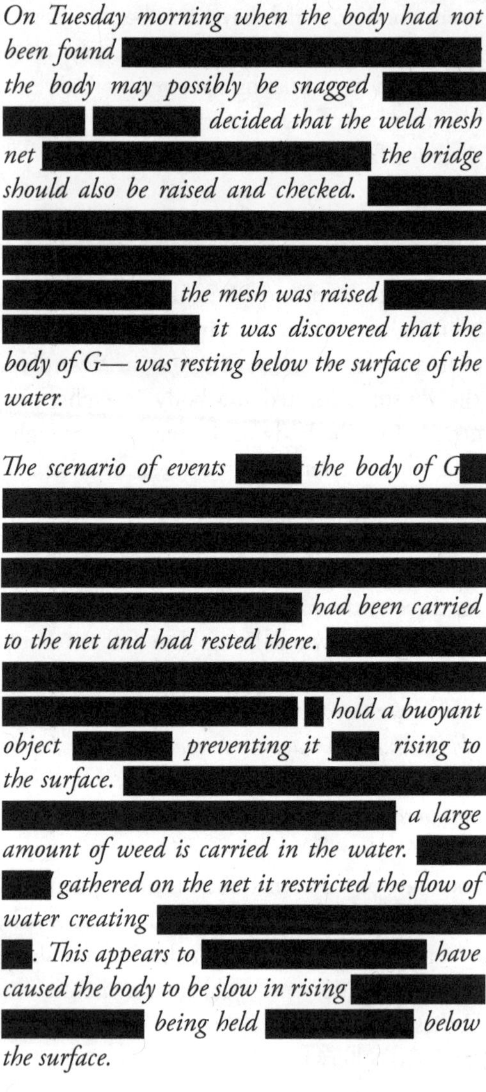

On Tuesday morning when the body had not been found the body may possibly be snagged decided that the weld mesh net the bridge should also be raised and checked. the mesh was raised it was discovered that the body of G— was resting below the surface of the water.

The scenario of events the body of G had been carried to the net and had rested there. hold a buoyant object preventing it rising to the surface. a large amount of weed is carried in the water. gathered on the net it restricted the flow of water creating . This appears to have caused the body to be slow in rising being held below the surface.

In those three days and three nights, how can we presume my brother's death? To do so is to imagine his absence as embodied. But in the death notices that my sister and I draft on the day before his body is found, we do presume.

That is what is written in his brief newspaper obituary—

Missing, presumed drowned.

I say my brother's body, my father's body, but what kind of ownership is there after the fact? Those left behind must claim and identify, bury, or burn. Must claim agency over them (these *remains*). If the body is no longer theirs, if *it's not him anymore*, then how is it still *his* body not found, left drifting?

Years later, my sister writes a memoir about the drownings. She titles it *Midnight Water*, the darkness of unknown places, of underwater opacity, but more specifically quoting Kenneth Slessor's poem "Five Bells" about the drowning of his friend Joe Lynch in Sydney Harbour in 1927. I first came across the poem twenty-two days after the accident; it is transcribed in my journal of that year.

The poem's speaker laments his friend, asking where he has gone. Time and tides have moved beyond the loss, but for the speaker, the memory of his friend and his death are stalled: a "flood that does not flow."

In her memoir, my sister traces her first remembered outline of our brother's body—

[G—] is still in the water. He will spend the night in the channel. [...] And [G—] in the water, left to drift in the dark, in the storm; that sinks in.

Once I saw an advertisement on the internet that utilised the artfully arranged depiction of a drowned woman. I don't recall what it was selling. The model in the advertisement is rendered exquisitely adrift, suspended upright beneath the surface of the clear water. Her eyes and mouth are closed. Her body assumes the obverse shape of the drowned position, face up, her back forms the closed arch of a horseshoe, arms outflung. Her skin is prettily pale as bone china. Strands of honey-coloured hair dance in transfixed motion around her stilled face. Fingers of muted sunlight penetrate the surface, framing her body as the mere simulacrum of a drowned woman, [Ophelia?].

Who would think to call Ophelia a corpse? She is but a woman emptied of herself.

What is a body, anyway?

Despite the gently poetic recreation of the journey of Virginia Woolf's body in *The Hours*, the salient facts remain that she entered the river on 28 March 1941 and wasn't pulled from the water until 18 April. Twenty-one days in that springtime flow. Imagine that.

The day after my brother's body is recovered, I ask the funeral director if I can see my father and brother. He answers quickly—*Oh, no! Best to remember them as they were!* I leave the room in tears. After I have left, my sister tells me, the funeral director goes into detail about what our brother's body looks like. If she passed on those details, there is (another) blank in my memory.

There are blanks in my memory.

(bang/flash)

When a person dies, or a body is found, the convention is to draw a cloth over them, over the body but especially the face. There is that sense of curtains (*it's curtains for me*) being drawn. Of borders.

US researcher Dr. Pauline Boss has pioneered a theory for what she calls ambiguous loss, or unresolved grieving. Boss claims that you must see for yourself that a person is dead—that breath has stopped—at the time of death or even when only bones are left.

Walking home from town on a winter evening in 1894, one of my ancestors, Andrew Spence, tripped over a mullock heap and fell into a deep hole on the outskirts of the ancestor land, Ngurai-illum Wurrung Country, of another ancestor, Dugald Cameron. Though he was rescued by a passer-by who summoned Dugald to the hole, Andrew later died in the house on Ngurai-illum Wurrung Country. The magisterial inquiry textually preserved his dying words, spoken to the other grandfather who helped pull him from the hole and took him on a carriage to his house—*Dugald, I'm cooked this time.*

Six years before his death, my father was having an after-work beer across the road from his Bendigo butcher's shop when he had a heart attack, aged thrity-nine. Other patrons were unaware for several moments of what was happening as he slumped across the bar, while he believed his life to be closing in on him.

In *The Guardians*, Manguso writes of photographs she has seen of the bodies of people who, like her friend Harris, were hit by a train. She writes of her research, how the matter of the body is squeezed out, red and yellow, over a larger area than you would imagine. She writes that after such a separation, there is nothing left to say about a body.

In a study written about the psychological effects on family members of viewing traumatically damaged corpses[2], one woman speaks about the death of her husband who jumped in front of a train. The woman says that afterwards, such was the catastrophic damage, there was no body left to retrieve. Railway officials let her climb down once to the tracks where the death had occurred, and she observed bloody fragments, shreds of clothing and flesh that had been left *in situ*. She located parts of her husband's St. Christopher medal. With no identifiable form of body, the woman found it almost impossible to believe it was her husband who had died, and not someone else.

After my grandfather returns from the channel, he gathers us from our various stations around the house and gardens. He wants us all in the house together for his announcement, but as we approach the front door he speaks informally, quietly affirming in an aside that my brother's body has been found. As my friend moves to embrace me, I slip through her waiting arms onto the gravel beside the driveway.

I'm happy to be taken, speechless, to the town's little hospital after the local doctor sedates me. Mistakenly, I believe the bodies of my father and brother are being kept here, too. From the bed I gaze listlessly through the slats of venetian blinds for a time until I witness a scene that I only later recognise as a hallucination. I see a gleaming black casket with a domed lid and hinged middle section lifted from a hearse onto a silver trolley. My grandparents walk solemnly beside it, dressed in black; the scene is imbued with the sense of the colours of my parents' wedding photographs from the late 1960s—those deep blues, those blacks and greys. My friend closes the venetians, and I think it's because she doesn't want me to look upon the casket. I slip into drugged sleep for six hours.

I have said that I read in the coroner's report that my brother's body was found *wedged* against a pylon under the bridge. And yet, at other times, I think I recall that the word used was quite different, that his body was found *nestled* against the pylon. The former seems to denote inertness, while the latter indicates a movement enacted with (impossible, departed) intent.

Nestled—a gentleness of word/image.
Nest—as if a home, sanctuary—
a resting place.
But perhaps I have made
this word up, this line from
the coroner's report, my memory of it.
Perhaps part of me is or has become attached
to this poetic image, this lineation
of his body being hauled up (which in some way,
it had to have been) like a *catch of shining fishes,*
or *dusky-skinned freshwater fishes,* or
other similar images I have used
to describe this moment.
Maybe it's a forlorn wish,
like the way my sister writes
that someone had placed a blanket over my shoulders
at the water's edge.

After my cousin cries *It's not funny*! *They're in trouble*! I run to my father's ute and scan it for something we might use as a lifeline. I find a hopelessly gnarled long length of orange nylon rope and run back to the channel bank. We lose seconds? minutes? trying to untangle it sufficiently to be able to throw. This is the way I remember it, but in my cousin's police witness statement, he recalls that he is the one to find the rope. He says in his police report that my brother made it to the dog, had hold of him before (he realised he was drowning). I have no memory of this.

In my own police witness statement, it says that after the policeman arrived, we (the policeman, and me standing, calling his name) continued throwing the looped rope towards the dog, over and over. I do not remember. I only recall the dog being pulled out by the State Emergency Service, the way he ran headlong into my arms when I called him, how I wouldn't let him go. How he was the only safe place left.

My laughter and my cousin's words, *It's not funny*! *They're in trouble*! These sounds do not exist in any archive. They are not contained in police witness statements.

The scene is full of noise, the crash and crush of water, and our quiet panic, but what is absent, what is already lost is at the very least, their voices. We never hear either man call for help.

They never meet our eyes.
They never look our way.

It is as though they have already left, or they are absent before they disappear.

Two years after the drownings I moved to Northern New South Wales. One day I travelled to the university in Lismore and browsed the campus bookshop. I randomly picked up a recently published book by Richard Flanagan, *Death of a River Guide*, a book narrated by a drowning man. The blurb on the back reads that the protagonist, Aljaz Cosini, immersed in the Franklin River in Tasmania, feels the water change abruptly in character from mild to murderous. I bought the book in a thrall of recognition. At the novel's conclusion, the tender mercy that Flanagan grants his drowned man almost brings me undone.

I lived at that time in a beach house fronting the Pacific Ocean, with five students from the university. On the balcony overlooking the beach one afternoon, one of the students was making up a story to impress a girl who had come over. I don't remember anything about the story except that it reached a point in the telling where there was a body in water, and then the body was pulled up in a fisherman's net. In a panic, I yelled at my housemate to stop talking, then burst into tears, and ran downstairs to my bedroom. The most distressing thing about the image he had conjured had not been its similarity to the recovery of my brother's body, but the realisation I had allowed myself to forget about my brother's body, suspended

in time,
in water,
in a net.

I have tried to immerse myself in the void that my father and brother vanished into when they slipped beneath the surface, to somehow inhabit that space, to be present, and to have fully borne witness. What is lost, unfathomable, is not only my father and brother, but what their deaths were like for them. How alone they each were in proximity to each other. In the company of others.

I laughed because I couldn't believe my eyes.

Because what I was seeing must surely have been a joke. Must have been purely performative.

DROWNED ON HIS BIRTHDAY.

Melbourne, February 17.

A sad drowning case occurred at Waranga Basin yesterday afternoon, when a lad, Charlie Cameron, lost his life. As it was his 16th birthday, he was allowed to drive out to the basin with his younger brother, and they had not been there five minutes when the hat of Mr. E. Corlas, who was standing by, blew into the the water. Young Cameron, who could swim, stripped off and swam in about 20 yards, recovered the hat, and was within a few feet of the bank when he called out to Mr. Corlas for assistance. Before he could be reached, however, the lad disappeared, and never rose.

We think of water as a familiar part of our landscapes, but it is like the binary of the inside and outside of our bodies in this respect, familiar and unknown at the same time. In many ways unknowable.

Drowning is popularly believed to be a relatively gentle death. Peaceful. That's what people say. I've heard it claimed as a preferable death to other kinds of deaths. Maybe if it had been a calmer sort of water in the irrigation channel, my father and brother might have slipped serenely from sight, the way I imagine Jeff Buckley dying in a slack-water channel, a tributary of the Mississippi River. His companion reported that Buckley had been swimming in the evening, singing Led Zeppelin's "Whole Lotta Love," and had vanished, been immersed without his briefly distracted friend noticing. Though no-one knows what Jeff Buckley's death was like for him. These are only words.

People don't just disappear. [Unknowable] things happen to them before that.

What I saw, and as Richard Flanagan, who writes from near-death experience, echoes in *Death of a River Guide*, was that the channel waters seemed personally bent on destruction, throwing, pushing my father and brother, thrusting their bodies down, only to have them surge up again with the force of barrelling currents, until the next downward shove.

Imagine
bloodless fingers grasping necks,
hands gripping shoulders,
pushing

d
o
w
n

grabbing at feet and ankles,
yanking violently.
Picture brute force.

The last time I see my father and brother, my cousin is in the water, having wrapped the end of the orange rope around his hand several times. There is no time for knots, for considerations of safety.

[no time to lose]

My cousin is midway across the channel, and I see my brother behind him, when suddenly my father's glistening body surges up from the depths, his arms held outwards, like Christ on the cross.

[*So, then, the duende is a force not a labor, a struggle not a thought. I heard an old master of the guitar say: The duende is not in the throat: the duende surges up, from the soles of the feet*[3]*].*

Then, he is swallowed.

Moments later, my brother disappears.

We never see them again.

Though their bodies are later found, they are forever lost.

In poems I have tried to enter that space. To inhabit the water in the same way Virginia Woolf's body inhabits the river in *The Hours*. In my creative writing honours thesis, a collection of poems about my father, I envision myself inside the skin of a stone on the bottom of the channel. I imagine my father's foot brushing the stone, his hair drifting like seaweed, his quiet face, his unseeing eyes peaceful beneath the surface of the water. I imagine witnessing from this impossible vantage, seeing the ending. Every moment.

In another poem, I picture my father drifting down through brown water saturated with sunlight, beyond time and story. The moment is cast in amber, the colour of his eyes, of his forebears' eyes, which he swims back through to join them. An honours examiner wrote about this image in her report, and my husband, who has not read the poems, bought me a ring with an amber stone to celebrate my success. I didn't have the heart to tell him that the amber the examiner's report referenced was a motif for the moment of my father's death. It's not as though I didn't already wear this moment, carry it with me.

Jeff Buckley's body was recovered after five nights in the water, when passengers on a riverboat spotted it caught in branches at the waterline. Maybe it was something, finally, not to be recognised?

Lost, as in irretrievable?

When I return with my boyfriend to the channel the day after the accident, there is a pile of rocks on the grassy bank. The mound is knee high, about two-thirds of the way down from the spillway, towards the bridge. It looks like a cairn, made of the slate-blue rocks that line the bottom of the channel, the same rocks you see underneath railway sleepers. At the time I assume that one of the searchers from the previous night, a policeman or State Emergency Service worker, or one of the police divers has built this cairn. Something to mark the place where my father's body has been pulled from the water, as thoroughly wet as my grey-skinned-broken-boned newborn daughter held against my breast in the moments after her birth.

Near the end of May 2020, the *New York Times* marked the first 100,000 American deaths from Covid-19 with a front page filled with nothing but the names and salient details of a thousand of the victims, the dense text mosaicked with details from obituaries of the dead. Each name marked space for a life lost, and for a body. By the end of February 2021, Covid's US death toll neared half a million. Another iconic *New York Times* front page depicted each of the many deaths via a single dot in a wall forming a dark murmuration of mortality.

My mother recently gave me a watch that had belonged to my brother. Once she gave me a little cardboard box that had belonged to my great-grandmother. The box has two drawers built into it, covered in paper printed with her family tartan, opened by tiny black ring-pull handles. A hundred years ago it would have held hatpins or hairpins. When I opened one of the little drawers, I found my father's wedding ring inside. I mentioned the ring to my mother. She said, *Oh, I wondered where that was. I thought it was lost.* She didn't ask for it back. I slipped the ring onto my finger. This is the closest I have come to joining my father or brother in the water.

In lieu of a body, there is this,
a plain golden ring.
An O gape?
Or widened eye?
Look,
it is empty now, but once—

My brother's watch is stopped at twelve minutes to four. A close enough approximation to a time of death, but I know he can't have been wearing this watch, as my father was wearing his wedding ring.

There is no
water trapped
inside the face,
no swelling
of the leather skin.

Seven years after the accident, I moved into an Art Deco flat in Elwood. My cousin's ex-girlfriend told me she used to live in the other downstairs flat in the complex of four. She said my brother had visited her there, with my cousin. My brother, his living body, had once turned from the street, walked deliberately up this same path; had stood on the landing outside my door.

Neither my father nor my brother ever calls for help. They appear inert in the water, upright, glassy-eyed. They never turn their heads towards our desperate cries. This is a source of confusion and mystery for years. In the first weeks, my sister and I stay up nights, talking about it, trying to work out why. As if answers might change the outcome. In this way, we begin immersing ourselves in the water from the very beginning.

About eight years ago I came across an article on the internet titled "Drowning doesn't look like drowning" by Mario Vittone, a lifesaver. The article illustrates a scenario in which a child is rescued from drowning right in front of her parents, who haven't perceived she was in any difficulty. In his thesis, referenced in the article, PhD scholar Francesco A Pia describes the phenomenon of the "instinctive drowning response." Pia lists the markers of this intuitive reaction. Among them is that a drowning person is too busy trying not to drown (too busy drowning) to turn their head or be able to call for help, that such a call requires breath, breath being the ingredient in such short supply. A drowning person is unable to move in any way other than the attempt to keep their heads above water. A drowning person looks as though they are trying to climb a ladder. The position is assumed by instinct, affect and biology. This is the instruction manual that a body follows as atavistically as the body of a baby knowing how and when to be born, and when to take a breath. A drowning person cannot reach out for a lifeline or rope thrown to them. Their limbs are no longer quite their own. Paradoxically, they have no more control over this response than they do over their body's imperative to breathe. Even if, being immersed, breath fills lungs with water, not air.

Birth is the inverse of drowning. To drown might be analogous to those liminal moments when a baby transforms from a water-dwelling being to one who requires air and breath. To go from non-being, to water, to air, and then at the end to make the reverse journey: air, water, non-being.

In *This House of Grief* Helen Garner writes about the trial of a man for the murder of his three young sons. The man was eventually found to have deliberately driven his car into a dam with his children strapped into their seats. Garner writes that everyone in the courtroom had to endure seemingly endless days listening to forensic evidence in which different scenarios were presented as to the sequence of events inside the car after it was immersed. How the water might have entered, how long it would have taken to fill all the spaces of breath left inside the vehicle, which might have been as long as nine minutes—time outside of time. The evidence of the elder child trying to save his siblings. In each hypothesis, how long it might have taken the children to die. Afterwards, Garner, harrowed, is unable to banish the thought of the imagined last moments of the boys. Her only buffer to the horror of the images is to picture the little boys transformed into water sprites, creatures native to underwater environs. She imagines all three escaping into a new *element* and happily continuing to live in a different realm of being.

I have taken to wearing my brother's watch. I don't replace the battery.

My brother studied graphic design in a mostly "analogue" way. Nothing he ever drew was digitised, or not in his lifetime. In the main, his body of work resides in a specially made large wooden box in my mother's shed. It's not a coffin, per se.

At a job that I began in the decade after the drownings, I recognised the graphics on the signage of the building next door as my brother's work. It is only in recent days that I have come to realise he also worked in this building in the year before his death.

On top of the butcher's shop in the town where my father and brother are buried is a large caricature of a jolly moustachioed butcher in a striped apron. It is my brother's sign, designed for our father's butcher shop in Bendigo. Later, it was moved here when this shop belonged to my grandfather and then my uncle. The sign remains more than thirty years later, looking over the main street of the town. A sign of life.

Another unconscious detail from my story "The drowned land" is the rain that falls on the open mouth of the dead boy at the end. But it's my father, my father's body that was found in the pouring rain. I think of the band Dragon's song, "Rain," its cautionary refrain not to go out in the rain, its recognition of endings—

When I dream of them, which is seldom, they are always silent. Sometimes they mouth words to me, as if still underwater. I have long since lost the sound of their voices. If someone lost their father, their brother today, those voices would be preserved somewhere. Someone would possess a video, or videos of them. Their voices would live on, disembodied, but present in some way.

On the day of the accident, I am writing a letter to my boyfriend. The letter bridges three days between the first and third of January 1993. The first half is written in red biro, a pedestrian teenage love letter to someone I have only parted from that morning. It is my before-life painted between words on the page, that is—

I board a bus in Inverloch and return to Melbourne after a week only to find public transport tickets have gone up twenty cents. I am so broke; I must beg for the difference under the clocks at Flinders Street Station. Back then I am not ashamed to beg.

The dry, hot summer wind whips my long hair against my face as I walk across St Georges Road after getting off the tram at the other end.

The letter continues into the Saturday afternoon. A complaint about another price-rise, this time the cost of cigarettes, which have risen to $4.90 a packet. I write from the sweltering interior of a borrowed caravan parked on the ancestor land, Ngurai-illum Wurrung Country. I write that it is thirty-eight degrees Celsius. The red part of the letter ends with a declaration—

it's time for a swim

VIC.

RUSHWORTH

The first time I write about what has happened is later that night. I can't sleep. To close my eyes is to view a loop of wide eyes, of open mouths, silence but for the sound of rushing water. The red pen letter resumes after midnight, but I have put aside the red pen.

The words from here are inscribed in fine, faint grey pencil.

There is a night in my life that is lost, known only through the stories of others. Each part of this story is told from a different point of view.

I am twelve years old. It is almost summer. I have been at Lake Eppalock with my father and my brother and his girlfriend. It's late in the afternoon. My brother, his girlfriend and I leave the lake in my brother's car. On the backseat beside me is a full slab of Victoria Bitter stubbies. My brother, nineteen years old, drives through a give-way sign in Bendigo and a car T-bones us on the passenger side. In my brother's version, everyone is knocked unconscious. My brother comes to first. He is uninjured. He wakes his girlfriend, whose arm is hurt. They turn to the backseat, see me covered in amber-coloured glass, and blood. They cannot rouse me. I go in an ambulance to hospital and don't regain consciousness until morning.

For years afterwards, my father liked to say that my face that night was a *bloodied pulp*.

This story my brother retells six years later, the day of his death. He talks in the car with our cousin and me. We are on our way to swim at the channel, earlier in the day, a different spot to later. He tells us how he had called our mother and said—*I've had a car crash. Dani's in a coma. Bye.* But in this retelling, he has reframed it as a funny story, leaving no space between the words—*I've.had.a.car.crash. Dani's.in.a.coma.Bye.* My cousin replies, *Lucky you didn't kill her, R— loves her kids.*

The iconic bodies found at Pompeii aren't really bodies at all, only visual echoes of what they used to be, the spaces that bodies once occupied, adumbrated with plaster of Paris.

My sister's first published story, called "Crystals," was written only weeks after the accident. In it she writes about the drownings, but also documents again that lost night, of how I answered her questions in the hospital, but quietly, politely, as though speaking to a stranger, and that later, I had no memory of it. My sister wrote, *[She] knew that she would not forget the image of her sister lying in the hospital, her body covered with blood and broken glass.*

Drown agony

POLICE praised the actions of a quick-thinking teenage girl who battled to save her drowning father and brother after they dived into a channel to save their pet dog.

Danielle Perry, 14, threw a rope to the men as they struggled against strong currents near Rushworth. However, her efforts ended in tragedy.

● Report, Page 6.

The black dog that survived the drowning was afterwards the saddest dog I've ever seen. There was a misconception among extended family and others that the accident was the dog's fault. The newspapers reported it this way. Even the coroner's report repeated this erroneous version, that the dog was first into the channel. Maybe because the dog was winched from the water in the presence of witnesses, police, ambulance, State Emergency Servicemen, the people from the nearby farmhouse. Maybe because he was the only one left alive in the water. It would never have occurred to me to blame the dog, but there was that narrative out there, this antipathy by others towards him in those days. In the days afterwards I didn't see him lift his head or wag his tail. Some months later, he disappeared. Like my other brother's dog, he was never found.

In the last photo of my father, taken on the day of the accident perhaps, or the day before, he stands on the ancestor land, Ngurai-illum Wurrung Country. He is wearing a navy polo shirt, stonewash jeans, brown work boots. There is a wide-brimmed straw hat on his head. He holds out a hose and the dog leaps off the ground to drink from the water that gushes high into the air.

The irrigation channel in North East Victoria that my father and brother drowned in is a man-made tributary of the Waranga Basin. The land beneath this was, or is a place called Gunn's Swamp, or Baangyoobine. When the Basin was filled via flooding of the Goulburn River in 1906 it was the largest irrigation project in the southern hemisphere. The land beneath was in some parts swampland, but people did live there before its immersion. There was a pub called the Cricketers Arms, traces of which can be seen in dry years when the water recedes.

The last line I write in my diary before the drownings is *It's been so nice.*

I have the 1992 staff diary from the Elwood video shop where my brother worked. It's full of good-natured, smart-arsed communications between staff members, some of them written by my brother. There's a note in there from someone telling him to tell me to rewind my videos (almost always *Betty Blue* or *Dogs in Space* that year, though my brother would also insist on educating me by making me watch movies like *His Girl Friday, Harvey* and *Suddenly, Last Summer*). The end of the diary continues into the new year. The second of January 1993 is the only page in that book that is completely blank, before the diary ends.

I did not believe that that day could end as it did. I possessed a childish belief that
a. bad things could not happen to me/the people that I loved, and
b. that everything would be all right.

I have lost this innocence.

There is an intersection in my own 1992–93 writing journal that reminds me of the boundary, the line in the earth that marks the border between the Cretaceous and Tertiary periods of time. It also delineates the geological event that, it is believed, caused the end of the dinosaurs. The line contains a concentration of iridium, a material found in large concentrations in the heart of asteroids. There is a crystal-clear border between

time before
time after.

In my diary, time before ends with those words—*It's been so nice.* In time after, the next page is blank except for two short phrases separated by a horizontal line, situated on the first empty page—

. . . the O-gape of [complete] despair

Please help me God

The next line in Sylvia Plath's "The Moon and the Yew Tree," after the *O-gape of [complete] despair*, or sitting on the same line, separated by a period and a space is the addendum that the poem's speaker lives in this space.

The memory of writing these lines is gone. Maybe I was writing from the space I occupied during the six days between the accident and the funeral, that interval of suspended time. Or maybe I was writing about what their mouths looked like in the water.

There are no waves in the channel, but the Waranga Basin is known to possess its own patterns of treacherous weather, of waves and undertows. There are no waves in the channel, but how do I describe the movement of water in that time, which cannot be replicated, encapsulated, or restored? How do I preserve the individual characteristics of a passage, a series of motions, [a suite?] of moving water? How do I inscribe the nuance, the shape and weft, grab and suck, the deathly motions of [those] underwater currents?

Every time I walk wet streets picking my way around snails, I'm reminded of my brother, who used to move errant snails from the driveway so he wouldn't run over them. In this way he is not lost but inhabits some other space of fractured being.

Several other men drowned in Victoria that day. [It is peak drowning season in Australia, those weeks after Christmas, a temporal no-man's land). A two-year-old child drowned in a spa. Other people's tragedies. Rudolf Nureyev died that week. All of this was as far away, as detached from us, as our normal lives and days.

There comes a time on the day they have drowned where I realise no one else knows yet, that my mother's life remains perfectly intact. My sister's and brothers' lives, everyone's lives are uninterrupted. They are unaware they are already

plummeting,

that our loved ones

have fallen.

DOUBLE FATALITY

TWO CHILDREN DROWNED.

MELBOURNE, Thursday. — A double drowning fatality occurred at Stirling's Government camp at Nanneella, four and a half miles from Rochester, last night. Edmund Hunt and Beryl Hunt, cousins, whose parents are employed in the camp, were drowned in the branch channel close to the main, Waranga Channel. Efforts at resuscitation were tried for two hours without avail.

Edmund Hunt was two and a half years, and Beryl four years of age.

In *Nox*, her elegy for an estranged brother, the writer Anne Carson sketches this impending approach of unknown absence and the intimately drawn shapes of time before its arrival; that while she was performing her everyday tasks, the news of her brother's death, which had taken place sometime before, was making its way slowly towards her, unsuspecting.

In August 1942, my twenty-one-year-old Great-Uncle Ronald died on a mud track near a village called Deniki in the New Guinea jungle on his second day of being a soldier in a war. The telegram to his mother arrived in Australia nine days later. In those nine days there were two versions of his body, the one hastily buried in an unmarked grave off the side of the jungle track, and the one still walking, breathing, talking—alive in the imaginations and hopes of those who loved him. During this interval, Ronald's mother, my great-grandmother, had her gall bladder removed. She sustained this wound not knowing until later that her body had been marked indelibly with absence. Her body, the scar, must stand as the only lasting (though not everlasting) memorial to her eldest child. Ronald's body was not recovered, though there is a plaque with his name on it at the foot of my great-grandmother's grave.

On the day my father and brother drown, sometime in the afternoon, perhaps between 3:00 and 4:00 p.m., my future husband attended his older sister's faraway wedding with a black eye. The photos of him from this day, conceivably taken during the same moments that my father and brother were drowning, show his body bearing this physical mark situating him for me inside a time, a day, an event that he doesn't know for years he has any part of.

When we depart the ancestor land, Ngurai-illum Wurrung Country, in my father's ute to go for a swim, my mother stays behind. In the time that elapses, she drives to visit a friend in the nearby town. Afterwards, she can't be located for a time. There are no mobile phones. Later, she says she had seen an ambulance speed past her, had noted—*Some poor bugger's in trouble*. She returns to the block of ancestor land, Ngurai-illum Wurrung Country, where she and my father are building their mudbrick house. When she sees my grandfather speed up the long drive in his ute, when she sees the cast of his face, she covers her ears with her hands, says *Don't tell me, Chief! I don't want to know*!

We all know the story of Schrödinger's cat.

Just before we depart for the channel, my father predicts rain, says
Storm's coming tonight.

Before that, we sit at the back of the twin shacks that, at the time, are still standing, in the remnants of the gardens on the ancestor land, Ngurai-illum Wurrung Country. I don't remember how the subject of remains comes up. But I know it's only my father and brother who speak. It's not that I've forgotten the words of anyone else. Nothing seems strange about this conversation at the time. It is only repartee; the words would probably have been forgotten but for what follows.

My father poses in front of the old kitchen mantelpiece of the ancestor house. He holds his can of Melbourne Bitter in one hand and a lit cigarette in the other. Says he'd like to be stuffed and mounted in this position when he dies. My mother snorts,

Who'd want you?
My cousin says, *I'd take you, Uncle Bob.*
My brother speaks up, deadpan—
I'm never gonna die!
We all laugh.

For a period after a person dies, the mourner's brain conjures an expectation to see their dead loved one walking in through familiar doors, like the doors of your home. In this way you expect a form of haunting, but they never arrive. The absence of their presence, the memory of their living body, swells and fills space until those thresholds shrink, and you come gradually to believe that they are gone.

A person is transformed in a moment,
they lose themselves, their body becomes
something else, transforming (falling?)
from body to cadaver.

In the absence of a body, the sight of a body, how do we make these translations?

When I finished reading Richard Flanagan's *Death of a River Guide* in 1995, I set the book aside and immediately wrote a letter to the author. I thanked him for the gentleness of his book's ending. I asked him if he had nearly drowned once. He wrote a three-page reply. In it, he said that he did almost drown once, and that writing *Death of a River Guide* had been in part an attempt to process that experience. He said there were parts he would probably never be able to write about.[4]

The speaker in one of the poems in Kate Middleton's *Ephemeral Waters* is told of the body of a boy who has drowned in No Name Creek, a tributary of the Colorado River. The body has washed up, has been found twelve days later (it is revealed later in the poem that it has been even longer than this). The speaker asks the reader to visualise what the body might have looked like after this amount of time in the rocky environment of the river. In marginalia this is followed by the words *sub-merged song* and a new stanza forms a lament in which the body is both "abraded" by the river's hard surfaces but is also in some way joined with and remade by the river. The boy's corpse is re-imagined as another component of the river's flow, its processes, transforming the body to also assimilate it. The body is simultaneously severed from soul and self, and imbued with a new spirit, at least as long as it remains part of the body of water that has ephemerally claimed it. There is an interval between the boy and the discovery of the body—days, distances that mark the intersection between the known body and the now strange, abject cadaver, no longer recognisable as the boy he was or even hardly human,

rewritten as he is,
by river and rocks and grasses.

[What kind of page is the body of a dead man? What do you write upon it?]

Julia Kristeva writes of the cadaver as a corrupted border that no longer holds back the abject, the concept of self as *cesspool*, expelling foul liquids, expanding and dissolving. She writes that the body has lost its designation as subject and transformed [translated] instead to object, and thus become borderless. To be without border is to be no longer able to conceal foulness—*ejected beyond the scope of*

the possible, the tolerable, the thinkable. It lies there, quite close,

but it cannot be assimilated.

We cannot love a corpse as we loved the person,
yet it's terrible to be separated, at first, from that vessel.

The day after the funeral of my father and brother, I remark to my friend H— that it is awful to imagine my father and brother deep in the earth, in that cold. I say to H—, *I know how Heathcliff felt,* meaning, I remember Heathcliff's refusal to give Cathy up, to give even the body of her up.

The only comfort I can imagine then is proximity, though their bodies have become unknown things.

(There is no assimilation).

Rereading *Wuthering Heights* years later, I am reminded of the actual lengths to which Heathcliff—not even slightly repulsed by the transformation death has wreaked on Cathy's body—goes, to rejoin the object of his obsession. Even years after Cathy's death, Heathcliff digs her up again, refuses all notions of borders, of endings.

I wonder if there was any portion of my brother's body that was not traumatised by immersion, was not traumatic. Was there any part left that was recognisable as *him*?

In Michelle Tom's memoir *Ten Thousand Aftershocks*, Tom recounts her experience of the Christchurch earthquakes, but also describes the deaths of her father, her brother and her sister. In each instance, she pays particular attention to the dead bodies of each, and to her levels of engagement with each. When the body of Tom's brother is found after a long period of his being presumed missing after his suicide (unbeknownst to anyone), Tom visits the site where the body was discovered. A policeman accompanies her and describes the circumstances of the body as it was recovered. The distressing condition of the corpse is described in detail to Tom, who writes that family members are advised not to view the body. Her mother asks if it would be possible to have some of her son's hair. On the day of the funeral, Tom's mother presents her with a small plastic bag of snippets of the hair. Though the funeral director has attempted to wash the hair, it still contains dirt, leaves, twigs, but it is recognisably *his—Him*. Something to hold.

My father's body is identified by one of his younger brothers. He must still look like himself then. At least, himself as object, not subject. My uncle later says my father has a slight smile on his lips.

Maybe it's not true at all, the part about the smile. I have never spoken with my uncle about it. Does the hint of a smile suggest a lack of suffering in the end? I am wary of the work of such translations.

Man and Youth Drowned at Waranga Basin

MURCHISON, Thursday.—At Waranga Basin yesterday, Ernest Wilfred Orr, 29, second youngest son of Mr and Mrs J. R. Orr and William Kennett, 17, a visiting relative, were drowned while bathing.

Days later, my father's friend identifies my brother's body. Afterwards, he has some very stiff drinks.

I read a paper about the pathology of what happens to dead bodies not recovered quickly from water. As I cautiously scrolled, I was unprepared for the sighting of an actual cadaver lying forensically alone on a gentle undulation of riverbank. Though I snapped the laptop shut, the image imprinted—the shape swimming, or floating, horrifically at first—behind my eyelids. (Julia Kristeva reminds us that in French, the word *cadere* means literally "to fall.") The dead have fallen to the state to which they have come/arrived, having "come a cropper," perhaps onto the page, the browser open before you.

The vision of the drowned man
inscribed upon my memory returns
and returns—
I recall the forceful push
of extruded lips, the tongue,
those thicknesses.
Each limb blooming with volume,
an idea that has expanded on the inside,
like breath with nowhere left to go.

I dare immerse myself again in the text, and stumble across more than one photograph, more than one drowned man. There are four or five, in different states of un-becoming and becoming, bodies unravelling into liminality.

There is no delicacy to be gleaned from the corpses of the long-immersed. You might limn an artless affect—the crimp of softened extremities, a *sloughing*—picture a body remade of wet tissue paper, unmade again. There is variation, of course, among the dead, drawn upon as much by surroundings, by circumstance and story, as by time and the original materials.

These words are a kind of body, but they're not
the same—
The soft violence of it, a folding
of the body as though inside out.
That kind of transformation. A lostness
of ruined flesh.
Horrifying, yes, but surprisingly
not unspeakably so.

When the funeral director refused me,
monstrous pictures appeared in my head.
They followed me from the room
and never left.

In the third of Michael Ondaatje's "Wells" poems from the collection *Handwriting*, the speaker points out that the soul is located close to the site of a wound.

My son's hair reminds me of my brother's hair, thick and a dark blond made up of strands of almost-copper, a sheen of bronze. It has the same dense thickness and appears light brown in winter when there is no light to reflect its many shining hues. So often, when it catches my eye, I recognise this trace.

In my short story "The drowned land," I wrote a few lines foreshadowing the later drowning of the protagonist—

He has touched the bottom before, soft, with a give like something dead, but it can only be reached with an effort of will that almost bursts your head. He will not attempt it today. He swims back up to the heat of the afternoon.

The student editor of the journal publishing the story suggested we change the wording to a reference to rotten fruit, as if even an allusion to that [other] kind of flesh was inherently offensive.

Various studies show that people prevented from viewing a body due to its damaged condition are often haunted afterwards by the spectre of the imagined cadaver, the horrible outlines of an unknown shape.

Historically, in Anglo-Celtic traditions the body was kept in the home until burial. It was washed and dressed by family members. It might lie on the family dining table, or upon a door taken from its hinges for the occasion. During this time, people would come to pay respects to the family and the body. Even children were involved in this part of the process.

In the past, bodies were commonplace. Death was openly acknowledged as a final rite of passage. Life and the dead were interleaves of the same story.

In 1955, after my great-great-grandmother died, my mother, a small girl, was induced to kiss her cold lips. This is one of the reasons we never view my father's undamaged body, which no-one was stopping us from doing, because my mother says that that forced (corpse) kiss meant that it was her dominant residual memory of her great-grandmother. She didn't want that for us. She wasn't thinking, no one was thinking then of what my last memory of my father had been. How, for me, a dead body might have seemed peaceful in comparison.

Though the form of the dead body, and especially the damaged dead body, is now taboo in Western cultures, this makes me wonder—what of roadkill? Those roads we navigate, where carnage is always spread, we encounter death in every shape and condition. We worry for the dangers posed by animals to ourselves, to our vehicles. We do not count the bodies, the horror of those casual decimations. These wrecked bodies are as benign and untroubling from a distance as the contents of my father's skilfully cut meat, the careful artistry of his showcase curations.

Consider, if you will, my father's showcase, or the showcase of any butcher you might pass by. Consider the layered scents, the garnishes of the interior. When I was a child, sawdust absorbed the viscous liquids on the floor of my father's, my grandfather's butcher shops. And a butcher clothes himself in darkest shades of blue, is adept at disguises. Is as mild as milk.

In September 2015, the world was transfixed by photographs of the perfect body of a tiny boy in a red shirt who had washed up on a Turkish beach. The drowned boy, Alan Kurdi, aged three, looked as though he was sleeping. Face-down, he seemed cushioned by wet sand. It was bearable to look upon this intact body as a motif for the refugee crisis arising from the war in Syria. The world could hardly stop looking, his red shirt an imperfectly formed semaphore, sending messages about bodies, their lostness, how they are vessels for everything we have to lose.

Near the beginning of *No Friend but the Mountains*, the Kurdish-Iranian writer Behrouz Boochani relates the story of a fellow asylum seeker travelling with him in the back of a truck in Indonesia towards a people smuggler's boat that they hope will deliver them to the supposedly safe waters of Australia. Boochani calls this man, a fellow Kurd, the Blue-Eyed Boy. The Blue-Eyed Boy has a deep fear of the ocean, stemming from witnessing the death of his brother in a river when the Blue-Eyed Boy was a child. Boochani writes that the Blue-Eyed Boy's brother's body was recovered two days later via the call of a "message-bearing" drum. Years later, the perilous journey on the badly damaged boat ends with the men on board being cast into the sea as their vessel is buffeted and finally swallowed by seawater.

Boochani describes his terror during these moments—dislocated from time, caught in a space between life and death, perceiving a malevolent spirit in the movements or "attack" of the sea. Ultimately, he is rescued, but it transpires that the Blue-Eyed Boy, like his brother before him, has drowned. So far away from home; there will be no *dhol* or drum, no musical relationship between death and nature to cajole his body back from the depths.

In August 2022, two Australian men of Lebanese descent flew to Lebanon to try to retrieve the bodies of thirty migrants from the wreckage of a boat that had sunk off the coast of Tripoli in April. They met a third man there who had spent some time living in Sydney. All the men were motivated by their own personal histories of being "boat people" as young children. Ten bodies had been retrieved from the boat on the night of the sinking. Those bodies left on the boat on the bottom of the ocean remained there. The recovery mission, funded by an Australian charity, made it possible to use a Pisces submarine to search for the bodies. The men said the images the submarine's cameras recorded were compelling, but ultimately the recovery mission had to be abandoned. The bodies, mostly those of women and children, were almost all beneath the decks of the vessel. When the submarine attempted to winch bodies that had been submerged in salt water for months, the corpses fell apart, and the silty bed of the sea where the boat rested was judged to be too precarious for further investigation. Instead, a ceremony was held at sea for the lost.

It is as though the sea, the river, all bodies, all bodies are water, are of water and will return, as the river returns to the sea.

The adjectives surrounding drowning form a lexicon that claims bodies as they fall.

Live bodies *spill* like water, into water, until that spills again into lungs,

the open cavities and soft tissues are flooded,

dead bodies *wash* up.

On the day of the funeral, six days after the deaths, we come as close to the bodies of my father and brother as most of us have been since the accident. As close as we will ever come again. The two coffins are covered in sprays of gum leaves and the yellow everlasting daisies that grow wild here. It is shocking to imagine my father and brother as obscured, as *contained* by the dual caskets. My gaze is transfixed, trying to imagine versions of the bodies I cannot see. I picture a papier-mâché effigy of my brother's dead body. He is a hollow object, layered with pasted newspaper typography, glossy magazine words. It is an easier task to imagine my father as resting in peace.

Into the caskets we have had offerings placed—

For my brother:

a bag of cherries,
his dilapidated childhood toy Mickey Mouse
made of faded cloth, the neck limp as if broken,
fixed with silver gaffer tape.

For my father:

beer and cigarettes.

In the church that my parents were married in twenty-five years earlier, we are speechless, though far from dry.

I am wearing a borrowed dress with long sleeves; it is the navy of a newborn's eyes, small white flannel flowers scattered across the fabric.

I wear my long hair down. I wear no make-up or jewellery.

In the car on the way to the church, with my cousin and twin brother and friends,
we play Van Morrison's "Gloria" up loud.

The two coffins are side by side, covered in yellow flowers.

The sound of sobs, my own and others, how our grief is indecorous, not coherent but inchoate.

I don't recall a single word said, or whether anyone speaks eulogies.

When the funeral cortege drives down the main street,
all the shops in the small town close their doors.

People stand outside and watch the slow procession.

At the cemetery, our unpractised keening sings the coffins into the cut earth.

My last sight of my brother's coffin is of the place where his face must have been, on the other side of the timber that obscured it.

At the time of the accident, I am reading Thomas Hardy's *Far from the Madding Crowd.* On the second of January, in the back seat of the car, I have reached the funeral of Fanny Robin. Sometime after, when I try to begin reading it again, I find I cannot pick up the story because to do so, I must first return to the scene of a funeral.

I remember again, the last time I saw each of them, my father, my brother—

glistening bodies,
glittering eyes. Wet mouths
wide as funnels—
and I wish I could know
what kind of bodies
they inhabited, then.

Physiologically, death by drowning is caused by massive multiple organ failures precipitated by water flooding and immobilising the vital functions of the body. I read that at a certain stage of drowning, a person will become unconscious, after breath has become an impossibly aqueous labour. A drowning person's body will finally take in water before they die.

One of the images captured by cameras from the submarine searching for bodies on the sunken boat off Tripoli shows the form of a woman holding a swaddled baby. Their bodies are suspended halfway out of a window that the mother has managed to break.

Swimming, we are always a body within another body, as though again inside the waters of our mothers' wombs.

On the afternoon of the drownings, though first to the water's edge and ready to cool down, I am the only one who never enters the water. Later, after the police, SES and ambulance arrive, when I am crouched in the grass looking for any sign of the bodies of my father and brother, an SES worker calls to me as though I am a small child, *Don't you get in that water.*

In the days after the accident, especially when my brother's body is still lost, I shudder to feel the flow of shower water on my skin, not knowing from where it might derive, and loathe to take any comfort in the movement of water. It takes a long time for me to be able to enter water again for the sake of pleasure.

Drowned in Waranga Basin.

The story of how Salvatore Cirillo an Italian POW met his death was told this week to the deputy coroner (Mr G. V. Furphy, JP) when the inquest was conducted.

Deceased was a member of a party of prisoners of war participating in a route march on January 7 and was paddling in the Waranga Basin. The recurrence of an intestinal complaint caused him to fall into the water and he died from asphyxiation caused by immersion in the water.

packing shed.

In his short essay "Out of a wild sea," about his near-death drowning experience in Bass Strait, Richard Flanagan writes that when people ask what it was like to almost drown, he answers that he felt a terrifying separation of body and soul.

In Thai Buddhist tradition, it is believed that after a person dies, the soul remains present until the body is cremated, and then the soul is reborn. Funeral rituals last days; they can last up to a year. When an acquaintance, a Thai Buddhist, died of the blood disorder thalassaemia, his body lay at the wat/temple before his cremation, accompanied all the time by friends and family. Repast was partaken of in the company of the body. There was music. Maybe even laughter. I am told there was no sense of revulsion or horror.

In the high country of Victoria, the week of the winter solstice, I walk home from school drop-off in the misty mornings. The bright grass underfoot crunches with frost, and I keep seeing dead king parrots beneath the oak trees. The birds appear completely intact, sleek green shapes, a different kind of gloss, more emerald than the grass on which they have fallen. It's as though they have died in their sleep, simply dropped dead. When they first die, the birds are still beautiful, as they were in life. At the beginning, even in death, nature continues to animate their forms. One morning on the way to school my daughter exclaims at the loveliness of gentle motion in the near distance: a coral ruffling, an innocuous softness. *Mama look! Something's moving there!* as though alive, but it's only the wind, animating a peachy fan of tail feathers, this bird having fallen on its face, having *come a cropper*, as Kristeva would have it. I wonder what could be killing them. Is it the cold? The long-fallen traces of acorns? Each day the green bodies fade, colour leaches from the feathers; the gloss and sheen diminish to brown. The shine that replaces that vivid green becomes something I begin to avert my eyes from.

In Jim Crace's novel *Being Dead*, the state of decomposition of the undiscovered bodies of two murdered protagonists—zoologists unsentimentally schooled in biology—is framed in language that weaves between unflinching depictions of abjection with its great ordinariness, the commonality between all matter. On a cellular level, our bodies are only composed on the premise of endings. Or we are composed with the biological understanding that we will inexorably decompose. As Crace observes, *Even stars must…*

In "Five Bells," Kenneth Slessor imagines the body of his drowned/lost friend as transformed—swallowed but also embraced, taken home by the sea. The body is refashioned, like the bones of the dead in the ossuary's of the Parisian catacombs, which become a single component of a larger whole.

To think of your own death, you must first think of yourself as a body. As nothing more.

The day after a friend's mother died in 2017, the friend asked her sister if she would like to view the body of their mother with her. The sister answered, *No, why would I want to look at a corpse?*

The cemetery where my father and brother are buried is one that I have always been familiar with, am fond of. There are perhaps twenty of my direct ancestors buried in this cemetery, aside from my immediate family members, and many more indirect relations, cousins, aunties, uncles of every remove. Crowds of family bones.

The afternoon they drown, my brother suggests that should he die, he would want to be buried here, on this ancestor land, Ngurai-illum Wurrung Country,
though he doesn't call it that.

It turns out it is a bureaucratic nightmare to be buried on private land, and my father's and brother's bodies are not buried on that ancestor land, Ngurai-illum Wurrung Country, though it seemed so important at the time to try to bury them there. It would have been impossible for my family ever to leave this ancestor land, Ngurai-illum Wurrung People's Country, if we had succeeded in fulfilling my brother's wish.

Wandering in the cemetery, my mother one day pointed out a grave to me that showed a date from the 1960s marking the burial date rather than date of death on the gravestone. My mother told me that this woman, in the knowledge that she would soon die, had walked into the thick ironbark forest between the ancestor land, Ngurai-illum Wurrung Country, and my paternal grandfather's slaughterhouse, and lay down there and died. My mother said it took weeks for the woman's body to be found, that the local townspeople had taken it upon themselves to continue searching the bushland surrounding the little town long after authorities had given up. Some weeks later, it was my great-great-uncle who eventually found the body.

My mother recalled another anecdote about this woman telling my grandfather in his butcher shop, *You can shove your leg of lamb up your arse!* But there is no context to the story, no connection except as the only stories I know about this woman, dead before I was born. Except that all the talk there is, is of bodies.

The woman's and my grandfather's remains both inhabit the same section of the cemetery.

When my grandfather was dying of cancer, a terrible, protracted agony, I witnessed his body's transformation as an irrevocable process, a sure trajectory. His bones were discernible through skin grown so thin as to be translucent. The flesh of his shoulders hollowed to shocking concaves. Emptiness colonised that space where once a big strong man had stood. Towards the end, to look upon his body, especially in sleep, felt like looking upon him after his death.

Or so I imagined. I have never looked upon a dead body. Unless I have.

Anwen Crawford's book *No Document* begins with a recollection of the beginning of the Georges Franju documentary *Le sang des bêtes* (Blood of the Beasts)—the slaughter of a horse, its metamorphosis from embodied to a body. How the horse's agency for movement becomes movement with nothing but the forces of gravity behind it.

A dead weight.

(Think of water. Of unseen hands shoving/pulling downwards).

Research shows that the foetal cells of babies remain as traces in the mother's body for decades after they have inhabited that space. This shedding of cells begins in the early weeks of foetal composition, so that even if the foetus is miscarried or aborted, some remnant of their presence will remain embedded, dispersed, floating within the mother's organs and bloodstream. I wonder if some dilution of the bodies of my father, but especially of my brother, remain on a cellular level as part of the flow of water in which they drowned, if their cells might have flowed all the way back to the Mallee.

In 1969, a meteorite shattered with a sonic boom in the sky near where my father and brother drowned. The pieces scattered over a wide trajectory, but it is theorised that the largest pieces fell into the middle of the Waranga Basin. This meteorite, a carbonaceous chondrite, was determined to be seven billion years old, much older than the sun. I saw one of the fragments this year in the Melbourne Museum. It looked as though it had been burned in a fire. What kind of ancient galactic particles might have leached from these fragments to colonise and infuse those waters?

Post-mortem changes are not only affected by water temperature, but also by current as well as obstacles and structures, both natural and man-made, that may interact with the remains.[5]

Walter Mikac, whose wife and two small daughters were murdered in the Port Arthur massacre in 1996, told Anh Do on his program *Anh's Brush with Fame* that after he had been informed of the deaths, his local GP arranged for Mikac to view the bodies in situ, before they were removed to a clinical setting. He says that this act of viewing was pivotal in his healing process, that the space for horror in his imagination that would have existed without it would have destroyed him. Mikac said that viewing the bodies in this state also left him with no choice but to accept the truth of what had occurred, papering over that chasm of disbelief.

Some years ago, my small daughter rescued a baby bird from the jaws of our cat. A quick internet search revealed it to be a pigeon, far too young and unfeathered to be a fledgling, surely too frail to live. There was a smear of blood on its head. It moved feebly in the palm of my hand. It was, I assumed, dying. I placed it gently in a hanging pot plant where it was safe from the cat, with the understanding that it would quickly expire. An hour later, washing dishes, I noticed a movement in the hanging pot plant and realised the bird was still alive. I took the tiny form and placed it instead into a shoebox with some fabric and put it where the children wouldn't see it. Every hour or so I would check on it. Each time, I was horrified to find it still living. How appalling to have intervened, to have prolonged the death. I wished I was more like my father, then, capable of doling out quick mercy. By evening, I was researching how to give it water, wary of doing it wrong, of drowning it instead. By morning, the bird had died. I placed it in the bin, casketed in its shoebox, thus shielding myself from having to look at that small body again, to see what would become of it.

My sister wrote a story called "The Sea-blue Background." It recounts how in the years soon after the accident, she and I both lived in places close to the sea but far from each other. She writes of the letters that we exchanged then, sometimes several times per week, and details a dream she once had—

All the mail falling out of the letterbox was from the dead. She sat down on the path and opened each piece of mail, but it never seemed to run out. The dead had written to her and sent her gifts from all kinds of places, every place they had ever been. But even though it was from the dead, the mail was never written or sent after death. The postmarks were old, years old. The mail had been held up somewhere, delayed, only arriving now, long after the drownings.

What kinds of archives do the waters my father and brother drowned in contain? What are their materials? Their contents?

Spillways.

bodies of water that push
outwards, away from the source.
Underwater weeds.
Prayers.
Blue slate rocks.
Orange fibres.
False teeth.
Teacups.
Lost hats.
Letters in bottles.
Children's beds.
Sharp grasses.
Dead everlasting flowers.
A variety of species of freshwater fishes:
Trout; Redfin; Golden
Perch; Murray cod, and carp.
Water insects.
Seeded bones.
Strands of hair, entangled.
Envelopes.
Unknown languages.
Carbonaceous Chondrite fragments
(older than the sun).
All the things we do not know
[endings].
The shape of the letter O.
Vessels.
(?)

These archives are elegies.

On Tuesday morning when the body had not yet been found

I know my father had swum in that place before, as a child. Before we left for our swim, he told us he had been swimming there every day that week. It's strangely comforting that he felt that water on his skin as a benign experience.

Carson's *Nox* is [also] a shroud or a casket (and what Carson calls an epitaph). It contains the (water-bound) ashes of her brother, the lost body of the ancient poet Catullus's brother, the limits of language. A border and an ossuary for these bones of memory, for what is known and cannot be known about not only her brother's life and death, but all lives, all deaths.

How delible are our traces?

Carson claims that *autopsy* is a word used by writers, historians and translators to describe first-hand knowledge. She says it is a kind of writerly agency, to piece experience together in this way.

I stand on the sharp grass
of the channel bank

as at an autopsy table,
returning again and again,

making small incisions only.
My eyes remaining tightly closed.

In 1921 in Palermo, Sicily at the end of the Spanish flu pandemic, Rosalia Lombardo died of pneumonia a week before her second birthday. The beloved child was handed that day by her father to an embalmer called Alfredo Salafia. The transformation that Salafia subsequently performed on the body of Rosalia was nothing short of miraculous. The body has been kept in the Capuchin Catacombs for more than a hundred years. Such is the state of the preservation that the body of Rosalia, laid out in a glass-topped casket, remains free of decay. Scans done without removing the body from its protective casket show that every part of the body is as perfectly preserved as it appears on the outside. Abjection has been kept in abeyance, but what is the cost of taking up this kind of space and gaze in the world once dead? What could it mean for the processes of mourning? Is there not also beauty in the idea of decay? Imagine that kind of haunting.

As living bodies, we are sixty percent liquid. Even our bones are partly aqueous.

Our organs mapped like rivers and oceans. If you close your eyes, you might see human bodies as always treading water.

MOTHER AND SON DROWNED.

On Thursday evening the wife of a settler at Nannella (Vic.), named Porch, was found drowned, with her son Stanley, aged 7, in a water channel near their residence.

The husband and wife were in Rochester, and returned home about 5 o'clock. The mother and two children went into the house, while the husband separated the cream. When Porch went inside he found his wife and children missing. He made a search, and heard a scream in the direction of the channel.

The father rescued the younger boy, aged 5, and succeeded in restoring animation. He subsequently discovered his wife floating face downwards, and the boy Stanley in her arms.

Studies into the benefits or otherwise of viewing bodies with traumatic injuries have found that most family members who have viewed a body do not regret the experience, even when the body is significantly damaged. After the 1987 Zeebrugge ferry disaster in which 193 people died, questionnaires returned two and a half years later by seventy-four participants showed little difference in the psychological well-being or distress levels of people who had viewed bodies recovered from the water in the first couple of days and those who viewed bodies recovered some weeks later.[6] The writers of the study remind the reader at the beginning: *Our society emphasises a need for order, with clear classifications and boundaries … a corpse may also feel dangerous because it leaks bodily fluids.*

I imagine pressing my forehead against the forehead of my brother, to show tenderness to a body made abject, but still, it's *him* I see in this fantasy, a face that I know. Would I know his drowned face?

The body of Emmett Till, a fourteen-year-old boy infamously lynched in Mississippi in 1955, remains one of the most enduring and iconic images of a body left immersed in water. Such was the brutality of damage rendered on this child by his murderers that part of the defence strategy during the trial was that the body, immersed for three days and nights, could not possibly be that of Emmett Till, but must be an older corpse, planted in the river by Till's family. Till's mother, Mamie Till, looked upon her son's body and recognised it despite the terrible state of the remains. She refused to let what had been done to her son be obscured. She was forced to have her son's body smuggled from Mississippi back to his home in Chicago, where she had an open casket. Photographers from *Jet* magazine took photos of the ruin of the child's body and broadcast them to the world as irrefutable proof of what people in the Southern states were doing to Black children in the US. The murderers were found not guilty. The body of Emmett Till was a huge impetus for change for the civil rights movement in the US. So enduring is the power of the photographs of the body, films are still being made about the lynching and its aftermath, books are still being written. In 2005, the FBI exhumed Till's body and compared its DNA to that of a relative. The body was determined to be definitively that of Till, laying to rest continuing racist conspiracy theories.

I watched a recent film portrayal of Mamie Till, now Mamie Till-Mobley, seeing the body of her child for the first time. In the film, she doesn't shy away from the transformation, no matter how terrible. As I observed the actress touch his toes and dare to still look upon his previously lovely face with her love for it still intact, I wept.

Some Buddhist monks practise deliberately contemplating corpses as a means of humility, a recognition of the transience of both life and the body. These monks are known to carry photographs of bodies in abject states to meditate upon. Monks have been known to meditate themselves to death and are recognised in Buddhism as not indeed dead but in the deepest possible state of contemplation. There is an uncanny tradition of the bodies of these monks being somehow impervious to decomposition.

The photographs of bodies from the Holocaust are inarguably one of the most shocking categories of text in existence. The shapes of such bodies, of tangled limbs in mass graves, mark the limits of language to express loss.

The bodies themselves form hieroglyphs. Untranslatable.

At Auschwitz, there remain enormous piles of human hair, literally tonnes of it, gathered in bales, the hair of the dead. The hair was originally used in German industry, as a product sold for money. Things the hair was used to produce include:

Thread (and fabric),
socks,
felt,
carpets,
mattress stuffing.

The hair is stored in glass cabinets at the Auschwitz Museum. Traces of Zyklon B found on the hair is seen by some to be the sole definitive proof of the murder of the Jews of Europe, though with passing time, the chemical traces have faded. Some survivors' families don't want the hair on display because it constitutes part of their loved ones bodies, the only part remaining. Others insist it must be on display, that it forms the single most powerful motif of the genocide. That one cannot look away from what was perpetrated when looking at these masses of human hair.

Also on display in the museum are bolts of fabric made from human hair. Products made by German manufacturers from this hair are believed to still exist in some German homes.

To look upon the hair in the deep glass display cases at the museum, even in photographs, is sobering. In some ways it seems more real, more anchored to people's living bodies than the photographs of the bodies themselves. In this way, it is easy to see why some Jewish survivors or their descendants would prefer the hair to be buried. Like the piles of shoes or prosthetic limbs, it is impossible to escape the connection, the visceral realisation that these relics are the actual remains of human lives.

In some of the camps the Nazis tried in the end to obliterate every trace of their atrocities, including the bodies they had buried in abhorrent mass graves. They had other prisoners exhume the bodies to incinerate, to obliterate, as though to un-write and erase their monstrous crimes.

In "Todesfugue," the Holocaust survivor and poet Paul Celan takes back, makes space for, these bodies even under the noses of the sadistic guards. The poem, Celan stressed later, makes a literal "grave in the air" for the murdered Jews, a resting place that cannot be touched by any further horror.

At Treblinka is a memorial composed of 17,000 stones of every different size and shape and heft. The stones are markers symbolic of Jewish headstones; they represent the missing estimated 900,000 bodies of the Holocaust murdered at that camp. When the Nazis *left* Treblinka, they levelled and buried the site, installing a farmhouse made of bricks from the gas chamber on top. To obliterate. Later, no bodies were found, but large masses of ash and bone fragments were recovered. Much ash remains sown in the earth, and the clear remnants of bone can be seen "especially after rain."

It is a Jewish tradition to leave stones on graves, to anchor the souls of the dead, to keep them close, and because stones endure. They do not wilt and brown and die. They remain.

After my thirty-six-year-old grandmother died of smoke inhalation in a housefire in 1963, my grandfather was given the wedding ring taken from her finger. Later, he gave it to his new wife.

My mother and I still talk about that ring. The stepmother is still living, in her late nineties. We hold out hope that when she dies the ring will be returned to my mother.[7] I don't know why it matters, but it does.

Victorian writers favoured beautiful iterations of dying, of "exquisite" corpses. Such versions of death stood as uncorrupted vessels, frozen in time, incapable of decay, preserved instead inside bodies of text. Bodies within bodies. But these bodies are fictional, composed always of only words. Only the paper on which they are written decomposes.

Even *abraded* bodies, *skinless* bodies, bodies on autopsy tables in fictional stories, in poems, in newspaper columns, are bodies made of words, only words, made of paper and ink. There is nothing abject about them, these bodies. Everything remains.

Five more drowned over the weekend

MELBOURNE: An 18-year-old woman tried in vain to rescue her father and brother who were swept away by fast-flowing water after they went to save the family dog, police said.

Danielle Perry's father, Robert, 45, of Northcote, drowned and her brother, Grant, 25, is missing feared drowned.

Police said Robert Perry got into difficulties after diving into water at Waranga Basin reservoir near Rushworth, 160km north of Melbourne, on Saturday to rescue the dog.

Grant, of inner suburban Brunswick, dived in to help his father and both men were pulled under the water by fast moving currents about 4pm.

Police said Danielle and her cousin, Andrew Perry, 22, tried in vain to rescue the two men using a rope.

The body of the older man was recovered early yesterday morning about 90m downriver of a sluice gate.

A search for the younger man was called off at 8am. Police patrols will continue to check the area.

Members of the Search and Rescue Squad rescued the dog.

Autopsies were performed on my father and brother. I remember being upset at the thought of it when we were informed the procedures would take place. There was no autopsy report, to add further details to the end of the story. No paper epilogues written of their bodies.

Writers Helen Garner and Lia Purpura have each written about visits to morgues. Garner's essay "At the morgue" draws a line between the life circumstances and the inert bodies she sees laid out before her. She notes that it takes repeated visits to learn that for the autopsy pathologists, there is little connection between the lives the bodies once lived and what they have become by the time they arrive on the cold steel of the table. In her essay "Autopsy report," Purpura evokes first a poetic rendering of a [drowned] body before her, and then admits to a faint sense of the absurdity of the bodies, as if interacting with a roomful of naked peers. On watching the bodies cut into, Purpura observes that this aperture seems familiar, not incongruous as expected, not terrible, if not entirely translatable. Afterwards, an incongruous tenderness follows her home, not in a haunting way, but as a reminder to be gentle with the living, those bodies she has seen transformed, all lives/bodies rendered so delicate, precarious, prone to sudden endings.

The Victorians, with their notions of beautiful death, also had their vogue for memento mori in the form of post-mortem photographic portraits. If you look through albums of these black-and-white photos on the internet, those whose subjects appear to be sleeping appear more poignant than disturbing. It is the photographs where the dead have been posed to look as though they are still living that are unsettling.

When Hippolyte Bayard depicts himself as a corpse in his 1840 photograph "Self-portrait as a drowned man," his portrayal begins with the slack tilt of the head and ends with an encroaching darkness of the face and extremities, but he has a face you can continue looking upon. His tongue is lodged firmly in his cheek.

The cemetery where my father and brother are buried is set upon a gently undulating slope of rocky, quartz-bearing land. The town proclaims itself *Gold and Ironbark Country.* My father's and brother's graves are among the older graves, at the top of the slope, by the far fence, beyond which is bushland, the largest remaining ironbark forest in the world. If you followed the road that their graves face, it would soon lead you to the mouth of the channel in which they died.

Sometime in the winter or spring of the year they died, there was a period of particularly heavy rain. After the rains, the mound of my brother's grave had visibly sunk. My mother warned me about it before I saw, but at the time I was unbothered. I wasn't thinking then about bodies, the state of them.

But there are intersections here, between bodies. My brother and the earth that holds him now enmeshed within itself; the channel waters, flowing within a coerced, unnatural bed, the grasses and silt also forming part of this body holding its own ground. When you begin to look for them, you find they are everywhere: the bodies, these textual forms, bloodless but undeniable.

This prevalence is not surprising—when you begin to pay attention, death is everywhere.

Yesterday, I showed my daughter photographs of Frida Kahlo's prosthetic leg, with its exquisite painted red boot, its ribbons and flowers. As an intimate bodily part once connected by straps and other nexus to Kahlo's flesh, it is a found poem, especially because it remains composed.

Of many of the early Norse (Danish) bog bodies recovered, the finders initially couldn't believe that the bodies weren't recent murder victims, so perfectly preserved were the remains that they uncovered. After the long compression of cool peat, the light of day destroyed many of these bodies. By the time the villagers went to give the bodies a "proper" burial in the churchyards, there was hardly anything left to bury. It's as though there is something magical, spell-like (or curse-like), in such simple biological processes.

I find myself contemplating the tenderness in the pillowy lips of the Tollund Man—those lines and creases, the slightly parted lips. After almost two thousand years, it is only his head that was selected for continued preservation. His lovely ancient feet have disintegrated beyond memory.

In Caravaggio's *The Seven Works of Mercy*, describing ways of caring for the poor, the part of the painting that depicts the mercy of burying the dead shows only the feet of the dead man.

In Sarah Moss's novel *Cold Earth*, one of the protagonists, Ruth, has recently lost her lover in a terrible accident. Ruth muses on the Italian linen suit that she wishes she could have buried him in. But, she says, his body has finished conforming to such conventional silhouettes, and at the time of the funeral was *no longer the shape of clothes*. Instead, Ruth keeps her dead lover's suit in the closet, next to a stunning dress that she used to wear, preserving their togetherness via the shapes their bodies once held.

In "Autopsy Report," Lia Purpura knows beforehand that afterwards, she will never look at bodies the same way again. In "At the Morgue," Helen Garner, standing before yet another corpse, comes to the realisation that while it is certainly … something… it is no longer what you could describe as a person, with all that is inherent in that.

A corpse is becoming, and un-becoming,
it is an in-between space,
known/unknown
body/corpse
person/thing
subject/object
flesh/meat
being/non-being
text/space
written/unwritten
rewritten.

THE DROWNING CASE NEAR ECHUCA.

THE CHILD IDENTIFIED.

BY WIRE.—FROM OUR OWN CORRESPONDENT.
ECHUCA, This Day.

The child who was reported to have been drowned in the Cornelia Creek was drowned in the water channel of the Echuca and Waranga Water Trust about 4 miles from Mr Simmie's residence. The channel runs through Mr Simmie's estate, and one of his boundary riders discovered the body, and it was removed to Mr Simmie's residence. On learning the name of the father of the child—a farmer named Anderson residing near the channel—he had the body removed to his [illegible]. Senior-constable Hallam despatched a mounted constable this morning to bring in the body to Echuca, where an enquiry will be held. The child, who is four years of age, was dressed when found, and it is supposed that death was caused by the child falling into the channel.

The relative coolness of water will allay decomposition, it will be slower than that of bodies left on dry land. Though there will be other damage.

Like Helen Garner and Lia Purpura, who have come before me, now let me pretend I am standing at a metal table, regarding the body of my brother.   No. Stop. Let me pretend it is someone else I am regarding, further away still than my brother. Let me pretend I stand before an unknown cadaver. This anonymous drowned man has many possible attributes—

the oft-described swell,
that balloon bloat
of skin made unfamiliar.
Washer(wo)men's hands
the crinkled
geometric pleat
of softened epidermis.
Goose-pimpled surfaces.
Sloughing of skin
[a sunken, sodden origami boat].
The purpled inscriptions of
lividity,
like channels, tributaries,
maps.

Not him,
anymore.

Let me pretend I stand first before a Pompeian
body. Mere space. Homeopathic distillations.

The faintest memory of a body…

I stand before bog bodies,
or the imprint
that a body has left in sand,
in mud, in plaster-of-Paris.
Let me pretend I stand before a space
and within it rests my brother's body transformed,
become completely abject. Become
what the funeral director saw.

Let me pretend
I stand before this space,
but that I am blind,
that translation might only take place via
fingertips. Such fleeting connections
might divine an understanding
I could bear to discern.

But all that is pretence.
There is no translation
but this,
these words.

My father's body, beside its blue
slate cairn, must have been more like Ophelia's.
Pale, wet, quiet.
His body in this state is an interlude.

A lacuna exists, existed between their bodies, the attributes of a corpse so changed at the beginning by those minutes, hours, days, nights—by the archives contained beneath the waters of the Waranga–Mallee Western Channel. The deceased body, before decay becomes evident, is a liminal space.

A corpse is not a poem, but a collection of words is all I have, to describe that absence, no matter how abject.

What would it be like to not have had the bodies, their corpses (unknown shapes) there at all? What if they occupied forever the realm of missing bodies? Large as a constellation, that kind of unexplored, impenetrable absence. That category of emptiness must grow larger by the day. I remember those [only] three days without my brother's body.

RUSHWO
ETORIA-H

RUSHWORTH
MILITARY FORCES

Though in other ways—less tangible, more slippery—we did not have the bodies. Did not have those final punctuations, though I know these are not the same kinds of absence as those bodies never recovered.

Twenty-one years after 9/11, the search for the bodies, for the identification of their traces—mere fragments—continues and will do so indefinitely. Just before the twentieth anniversary of the attacks, the remains of an unnamed man and of a woman, Dorothy Morgan, were identified. More than 22,000 unidentified stored body fragments remain. It is now DNA testing that forms the basis of yoking remains to identity.

My mother was contacted last year by the Queensland University of Technology. A research project is underway to identify bone and other material fragments from World War II bodies recovered from the jungles of New Guinea. My mother has sent a sample of her DNA, which will be used to try to identify the remains of her uncle, a soldier who was killed in 1942, should any of these fragments belong to him. I try to explain to my mother the matter of bones, of remains, that the best we can hope for is a trace of the body, a small piece of bone perhaps, nothing more. Though any trace of his body is precious to us. What is it that is so emotive about bringing a body home, of laying it to rest?

People jumping from the burning towers on 9/11 were described as being like angels—as ephemeral and incandescent and endlessly storied—as that.

The Polish poet Wisława Szymborska writes in "Photograph from September 11" of an image of those bodies transfixed in the air, their blood for now concealed. The poet claims that two things are granted to the stilled bodies via this image: first, the inscription of their fall written on sky and second, the allaying of their inexorable end. Pinned like butterflies, the bodies remain captured. But not just in the image that Szymborska describes via her words, she has also transformed the bodies into a poetics.

In "Leap," the writer Brian Doyle does describe the end. He untethers the bodies from their state of pinned falling-ness—by describing a pink mist that the mayor of New York City reports on the day. Doyle returns to the unfinished-ness of an unidentified pair who leapt from the towers holding hands. He holds with the moment of this tender intimacy between strangers (or friends or colleagues, it is impossible to know)—what bodies could do in a captured moment of hope and faith and in the certain face of a terrible ending.

In Flanagan's *Out of a Wild Sea*, when the writer felt there was close to no hope of being saved from drowning, he caught sight of an island not too far away, and he kept trying to reach that island. When he was saved, he asked his rescuers how far they were from the island. His rescuers thought him mad from his ordeal, explaining to him that they were many, many miles from land.

None of the people who leapt to their deaths on 9/11 were ever identified. To this day no one knows who jumped.

There is a time, earlier in the day on which he will later die, that my brother, my cousin and I swim in a different part of the channel, a part that we all know and have visited before. The three of us leap from the outer side of a bridge known as Fraser's bridge, all together. We let the swift currents sweep us only a little way downstream before we cut across close to the weeping willow and then we get out and jump again. This sequence feels endless. On one of our jumps, my brother claims to have landed on something large and hard, maybe a log or a branch hidden beneath the surface. He will not jump again, though we try to convince him he has imagined this hard landing, this sense of danger. We point and gesture towards the water, the lack of obvious obstruction, the fact that we were right beside him and felt nothing. My brother is unconvinced. He refuses to join us and after my cousin and I jump into the water another couple of times, we leave, and return to the ancestor land, Ngurai-illum Wurrung Country.

I freeze the moment
my brother leaps
from the bridge.

I transfix him. Imagine him

safely pinned,
an image stalled
before the fact, before

he disappears.

The body, this body is only a word, only

lines, text.

It cannot drown.

[No one would presume that a butterfly, pinned, preserved this way, is the same as one in flight, resting on a flower. Though they form doubles, of a sort.]

In *The Guardians,* Sarah Manguso writes that two nights after the attacks, it began to rain in the city. She says the bodies started decomposing faster, though I wonder how she knew. I wonder if this was what people were thinking about then. Not only of the missing and the dead, but of the states of their bodies.

Fewer than one hundred of the victims' bodies were identified in the immediate aftermath of 9/11, though other sources say 292 bodies were found, and fragments from another 1,357 bodies were recovered. Such details are everything and nothing combined. The remaining bodies were considered by experts to have been entirely consumed or destroyed by fire or crushed by the massive weight of building materials—unrecoverable in any way.

For me, it took a lot of time to reimagine my father and brother's bodies as dead. Though in the days between the deaths and the burials I heard the second-hand stories of those tasked with identification, still I had a complete failure of imagination.

It's not him anymore is a body of words. A vessel. *(*Empty.)

I don't recall seeing my brother enter the water below the spillway. I think it coincided with the indelible picture of my father's body cascading over the lip of the fall. I must have had my back to my brother then, after telling him, *The dog's in the water.*

[I imagine the sight of my own body as seen from afar, a slight figure in black bikini, witnessing her father dive in and the dog follow suit, this girl calling to her brother the words that propel him into water, and then the way her father falls—is propelled—over that gushing downward flow. As if I am standing centre stage beneath a stark spotlight before the scene turns away again from me.]

It is not until the body of my father has surged up through the turbulent surface, just before he goes under again for the final time, that I see my father and brother in the same frame. Though they seem miles apart, with my cousin between them, also miles away from either man.

And me so far from any of them.

The width of the channel, the spaces between each of us, are in memory, impossible distances.

However, her efforts ended in tragedy. 8

Drive past any forest in Australia and imagine all the places that could harbour a body. The denseness of a thousand forests, a hundred thousand lonely paddocks. Lost places, forlorn ground. The bones of landscape and of Country. How many bones do we dwell upon? This land that we occupy is a palimpsest. The ground is haunted with blood and what remains unwritten. Histories. Reckonings, and the lack of them All buried.

Across Australia, there are more than five hundred sets of unidentified bones in morgues and other storage.

Spanish poet Federico García Lorca was assassinated in 1936 at the beginning of the Spanish Civil War. His body has never been found. His niece has stated that wherever her uncle's body is located is a sacred place by virtue of its practical designation as a grave; that it doesn't need recognition as the burial ground of a famous person to be a suitable resting place for her uncle.

In her essay "The Dead Still Among Us" Deborah Lutz claims that to the Victorians, the materiality of the relic—the ubiquitous hair jewellery and trinkets— not only represented the preservation of memory but also provided a direct link to the dead, to a continuing manifestation of body and presence.

In the New York Holocaust Museum, unlike the Auschwitz Memorial, the tonnes of preserved hair are not physically displayed but represented via photographs.

What is abject about the body of a dead star? It is so easy to look upon that kind of emptiness.

Walter Benjamin calls generations who had never slept in houses with rooms that had also felt the weight of a death, *dry dwellers of eternity.*

I write this with my computer on top of an inherited wooden table. This ancestor table of mine is so old, there is no way of knowing if the bodies of my forebears were laid out upon it.

When a close friend's beloved stepmother J—, an artist, died of cancer in 2019, she was able to spend her final days at home. When J— died, her body was tenderly wrapped in a beautiful shawl before she was taken away from the former bedroom of her deceased daughter, decorated with J—'s art. Later, her women painter friends, a group she had known since her youth, painted colourful images all over her cardboard coffin. Her funeral service was filled with rambling anecdotes and her paintings; renderings of sky and clouds especially were placed all around, as if a gallery.

I think of my great-grandmother living always with the memory of her drowned cousin, that early trauma. My great-grandmother at eighteen, the same age as me when my father and brother drowned. The body of her cousin would have been laid out in the darkened front room of that house that seemed so spooky to me as a child: no electricity, still lit by oil lamps even then, in the late 1970s. I imagine his mother, his grandmothers and aunties, perhaps my great-grandmother too, all gathering to tend to him inside this house. I wonder if afterwards, those women were haunted by the sight of the boy's drowned body. Or if it was the opposite of that, that the engagement with his body laid his ghost to rest and those who loved him might live only with the other losses, those of his presence rather than that of his body. I imagine how they all got to bid farewell, with last touches of love on his closed eyelids, his lips. Last glimpses.

Though my imagination in this matter is a story. A page, a line. Though it might have been awful for them. Though they might not have been able to bring themselves to look upon his damage at all. These words I write cannot constitute a body. They do not lay hands or eyes upon a body.

In these circumstances, is a corpse a panacea? I don't imagine so. My great-grandmother was still speaking of this death in her nineties. There is a thread, a line that runs between bodies and stories.

In the 1800s, a well-preserved body was uncovered in Denmark. The body had long, glossy brown hair and was believed to be that of a woman. The body had been held down in the bog by means of many forked branches. The local people understood the idea of restricting the movement of the dead. A related article from that time describes the recognition of the woman's body as someone who had been considered a witch in their own time, and that measures had been taken to stop her rising from her grave after death.

Bodies were recovered from Danish bogs for hundreds of years. These bodies retain a certain poetic grace. Nothing is known about the identities of the dead, and so they are deemed not to be individually significant in a historical sense. They, or their bodies, are only historical insomuch as they remain (randomly) so remarkably well preserved, and so they come with the possibility of stories still attached to them, like trailing umbilical cords.

In his 1975 collection *North*, the Irish poet Seamus Heaney links images of the ancient world with Ireland's contemporary Troubles. He connects some of the more renowned Danish bog bodies to the present. Of the Grauballe Man, he ponders the uncanny powers granted by preservation, and by the distance of time.

The poem's speaker asks who could address such a figure as *corpse*? How could anyone reduce the image of this mysterious slumber to that of mere *body*? The poem stresses that it is preservation—a retained sense of if not beauty then recognition of humanity—that keeps revulsion and horror at bay, imbuing in the form an almost magical quality instead.

The poem stresses that it is preservation—a retained sense of if not beauty then recognition of humanity—that keeps revulsion and horror at bay, imbuing in the form an almost magical quality instead. The poem concludes, however, with a return to the prosaic—what Heaney refers to as the *actual weight*[9] of knowledge, that the bog bodies are not mere curiosity, nor just tangible traces of history, but that they form the shapes of actual bodies, were once living forms. Individuals who were led, hooded, to their violent and opaque deaths.

Their bodies form those shapes, punctuations of their terror, their suffering, their endings.

Lorca presciently claimed *that a dead man in Spain is more alive when dead than any place in the world.*[10] The presence of absence has surrounded the body of Lorca in such a way that the search for his grave has been constant since he was murdered in 1936. The idea of his body has never faded, is bright as a blank page.

In the film *1917*, the protagonist almost drowns in a close escape from German troops in France. The young soldier's body emerges from a dangerous flow of water into a gentle stretch, where he reaches a floating tree branch. The soldier clutches the branch as a lifebuoy but is so weary he momentarily loses his grip and slips into sleep or unconsciousness. His body lies supine just beneath the surface of the water as though having succumbed to death before he splutters back to life and breath. He strikes out for shore, but to reach it, he must struggle through the bloated corpses of dozens of fellow soldiers. These corpses represent not merely dead but abjectly dead men, albeit only mildly so, a sobering representation, yet still palatable, acceptable for a mainstream film audience. The cadavers are after all *contained*, less a modest scattering of extruded tongues, but these figures too are poetics, words on a celluloid page; are rendered textual tropes of dead men in water.

The kinds of textual tropes that might rise unbidden in your mind when a funeral director tells you that it is best to remember the dead as they were.

Is it unseemly to represent the abject dead?

Is it irreverent?

In 2009, in what was expected to culminate in the exhumation of Lorca's [mass] grave, no cameras or mobile phones were allowed, so that no images of Lorca's remains might make their way to the internet, become digital currency. The grave turned out to be empty, to be no grave at all. Lorca's final resting place remains unknown. Lorca's niece, the head of the García Lorca Foundation, claims that Lorca's grave should not be elevated above the graves of the many other unknown burial sites in Spain.

It is one thing to embody the dead as text, as textual, as a poetics—I don't suggest we throw open the morgues. I don't recommend looking up photos of drowned dead men, but as I write today, a video of the death of the victim during a shark attack in Sydney, of his instantaneous transformation from man to body parts, is circulating openly via some news outlets. There are trigger warnings. Such is the reverence for bodies in the internet age.

The corpse is a punctuation. A kind of type. A hieroglyph. If elegy forms a refusal to give up the dead, the body is a page we begin to inscribe.

But the drownings of these two men are written upon my body. Grief will change the composition of your cells.

Composed, we are water.

Is any body translatable?

For the dead that Paul Celan has known and the vastness of those he hasn't, whose personal fates remain unwritten, there are no words to contain their bodies, to atone for the unspeakable void of those losses. That elegy is empty. There is no consolation of ritual. In "Nocturnally Pouting" he writes of the contrast between writing of the dead and being able to physically tend the dead. Implicit in the lines are the inadequacy of the former.

In 1945 when the United States dropped two atomic bombs over Japan, Little Boy in Hiroshima and Fat Man in Nagasaki, there remained over both cities what are called nuclear shadows. When an object has absorbed the nuclear blast and has effectively shielded the surface behind or beneath it, nuclear shadows occur. These spaces are preserved as white against a dark background. In Hiroshima and Nagasaki, these shadows were sometimes all that was left of the people or animals who had stood in the path of the blast. It is believed that in the immediate aftermath of both bombs, there were many more of these imprints than could eventually be preserved, that subsequent blasts of thermal energy and fire erased most of the shadow remains. The Hiroshima Peace Memorial Museum displays a small set of tiled steps from the entrance to the Sumitomo Bank. The nuclear shadow of a sitting person remains on the steps. According to the museum's website, several people have claimed to know the identity of the person whose imprint is held there, though this can never be confirmed.

The bodies of the dead don't occupy white space so much as they have become the white space.

A corpse might be a vessel for poems, too.

A repository for other people's memories.

In her poetry collection *Cadaver, Speak*, Marianne Boruch conjures a poetic speaker, the corpse of a ninety-nine-year-old woman, who guides the reader into her own dissection. Spanning many pages, the speaker in this poem veers from wry humour to pathos to beauty in the company and observation of both her three fellow cadavers, and the medical students who are tasked with taking apart the bodies. The old woman's cadaver casts a temporal thread between the seams of her life and the visceral unstitching that is taking place in the present.

To write this collection, Boruch, who has been a writing and literature professor for many years, took up the opportunity of a fellowship at her university encouraging applicants to undertake a semester of study as far removed as possible from their usual endeavours. In her proposal, Boruch suggested she should attend to embodiment via both the pathology lab and a concurrent life-drawing class. In an interview about the process of writing *Cadaver, speak*, Boruch says that the four bodies in the anatomy room were dissected first from their backs—that is, their spinal cords were removed. The head anatomist said the back was the least personal part of the body (easing the students in). Throughout the semester, the heads and faces of the cadavers were wrapped "like mummies" in moist cloth. It was only at the very end, when all the other parts of the body had been progressively dissected, that the faces were revealed. Boruch says that when she saw these faces, she found them quite beautiful. She realised that it wasn't just that the face was the most *public* part of the body, but that it was the most *private.*

I remember a throwaway comment my brother made watching TV one day in the year before he died, about how beautiful he found Madonna's back.

What stories did my father's body tell the people who performed his autopsy? It must have been a very different story to that which my brother's body told. Less detail, the stories stored in dwindling silence, inaccessible to the scalpel. There is no record of these narrative, or not ones that I am aware of.

ANOTHER RURAL TRAGEDY.

MOTHER AND CHILD

DROWNED IN WARANGA CHANNEL.

ANOTHER CHILD RESCUED.

ROCHESTER, Friday.

A shocking drowning case occurred at the Nanneella Closer Settlement last night, when Lucy Porch, a settler's wife, 47 years of age, and her son Stanley, 6½ years, lost their lives in the Waranga channel.

Mrs. Porch, with her husband and two children, were in Rochester yesterday doing their shopping. On arrival home at about 6 p.m. the parents milked the cows, after which Mrs. Porch went to the house to prepare the tea, taking the two children with her, while the husband stayed behind to work the separator.

On going to the house about 8 p.m. Mr. Porch missed his wife and children. Hearing a scream in the direction of the channel he rushed to the spot, and found his youngest son, five years of age, floating face downwards in the water. He rescued the child, who was then unconscious and eventually brought him round.

Then the father made a search for his wife and the other boy. He found them several yards further up the channel, in several feet of water. Both were dead.

The police and Dr. C. R. Lease were summoned from Rochester. A medical examination showed that both the victims were dead before

How are their bodies archives?

I rewrite, I rewrite, I rewrite.

Is not the corpse itself the elegy for the body that preceded it?

In *On Earth We're Briefly Gorgeous*, when Ocean Vuong's grandmother Lan dies, the writer helps prepare the body. Vuong draws the line between what was and what is. What he once called Grandmother he now calls corpse. But the old woman/corpse in *Cadaver, Speak* worries not about such distinctions, knowing that to be one is to be the other, or to be one is to have been the other.

As a cadaver, she sees how seamless that intersection is—two sides of a leaf.

To imagine still loving my brother in his drowned-man form, I must think of him as no-longer-*him*-at-all. To think of him in this fleeting form from long ago is to temporally suspend him as newly dead. As *recovered.* As if his body in this form has no future, only these days between recovery and burial. The idea of him in this state is as if he is suspended in amber.

To view a body, to imagine it viewed, these are acts of translation.

Though, the closer I draw to these bodies, the further away I get.

The deaths of my father and brother take place in running, fast-flowing water. The actual locus of each drowning only exists at the moments of their individual deaths and then they, these sites, have passed, are moving, lost, unmoored, words written in water. The area of my witnessing, in contrast, is fixed—the physical structures of the spillway, the engineering that underpins the passage of water, these are concrete sites. You can lay yellow everlasting flowers there, in that place where I stood.

The places they were each found—
Cairn/bank.
Net/bridge.
These are tangible
end points,
periods.

I recently read Audrey Maggee's novel *The Colony*, which details what happens when an English painter and a French linguist converge with the native occupants of a remote Irish island in 1979, while elsewhere, the body counts on both sides of the Troubles pile up. I was most affected by the character of Mairéad, one of the island's inhabitants who has years earlier lost her fishermen father, brother and husband to drowning, their bodies never found. Mairéad contemplates the sea and imagines what might remain of her husband within its vast reaches. She wonders if there are any material parts of him left at all, or whether he has become mere particles, motes of light or matter, moving through ocean currents, travelling the world. Mairéad stands by the sea for years and years, waiting for her love to return to her, even knowing the impossibility of such a reunion. I cannot pretend to imagine the fathomlessness of a sea grave, the ambiguity of that brand of unfinished grief.

A. E. Stallings' poem "Refugee Poem" reminds its reader that to fathom is to "hold within your arms."

At the bottom of Portsea's Cheviot Bay in Victoria is a sunken gravestone for Harold Holt, the missing, presumed drowned former Prime Minister of Australia.

I have written that the red-lettered part of my missive on the day of the drownings ended with the words *It's time for a swim* but when I fish out the actual document, I see I have misremembered. The letter ends instead with an ellipsis. *It's time for a swim*[11] is an invention (an intervention) of memory. The actual words read—*Oh God, it's so hot! I want to go back to the channel now [...] But in any case, this caravan is very unpleasant, so I'll go, and I'll continue this later ...*

There is a gap in my memory following this moment. Time jumps from the interior of the caravan I am sitting in, sweltering in, writing the letter—I think of the worn DVDs that my son plays over and over, the way they skip unevenly to different sections—so that my recollection jumps from the caravan to a still scene showing a large gumtree that my father's yellow ute is parked underneath. We are all—father, brother, cousin, girl, dog—getting into the ute to go for a swim. We are embarking on our journey to the channel, the spillway. My father looks up at the deeply blue sky, at what I see as fluffy white clouds, and he predicts an impending storm. I scoff at this prescience, as I am wont to do at that age.

The day is so hot,
so blue.

By the time the storm arrives, the police have already begun to search for the bodies of my father and brother. They search through the storm, until they give up and leave my brother to the opaque water.

I am the one who has suggested the swim. It's me who has at least thought those words,

It's time for a swim.

The one who has written in red ink (indelible?)

I want to go back to the channel now.

My idea for us to travel to this town for the day in the first place. I have placed us here, together.

[I have no other space within which to hold together these scattered wounds.]

My father's family tell stories about him in which I hardly recognise him. I can lay no claim to these versions. My uncle shows me the place where, as a mischievous child, my father carved his name into the family table. This trace remains of my father as he was, long before I knew him.

When we knew for sure that our son was profoundly autistic, we had to shrug off everything we thought we knew about our lives. This is what it's like when something huge shifts. You must be humble in the face of your ignorance.

I think also of my brother, how incomplete anyone's told or remembered version of him is. I cannot impart the spirit, the meaning of him through my words, though he seems complete and [almost as if] living in my head. Though that is also untrue. He is a series of static images, a collection of memories, motes that rise and fall with the light. He is silent—I have lost his voice, the fluidity of his movements, the way he walked, and laughed. I think of Nick Cave's words about his dead son Arthur in Andrew Dominik's film *One More Time with Feeling*. Of how his son lives in his heart, but that also he is not there at all, that that is nothing but words, a thing you say [to fill a howling space].

How unknowable they are, the dead. Unreachable.

I open a box, a green chest in my mother's shed that shoes were once kept in and find my brother's HSC[12] windcheater from 1985. I am astounded by its smallness. It appears made for a child, as though it would fit my ten-year-old son. My mother and I wonder aloud if perhaps it belonged to someone else, a girlfriend, perhaps? My brother was six feet tall, but seeing this item of his clothing, I begin to question everything. This is the only item of his clothing I have seen in many years.

I kept an unwashed T-shirt of his after his death. I slept with it until it lost any remaining scent of him. The whites yellowed.

Anne Carson's translation of Sappho, *If not, winter*, recreates Sappho's work mostly via its elisions. The body of work is vastly composed of what no longer remains. Of white space. Carson must work with the fragments of the known—precious little.

Fragments grow less with time.
Slip away.
Disappear
into white spaces.

The inscriptions on my father's and brother's gravestones contain their names, the dates of their births and deaths, and on my father's grave, the words *Our one and only bush-tucker man*[13], and on my brother's grave, *My darling Granty boy.*[14] The words are not words we ever used when they were living, but being etched in stone makes the words, their sentiments, seem irrefutable.

Only years later do I realise that in his death notice, my sister and I have added five years to our father's life. No one points it out at the time. Does anyone even notice?

In the journal that I kept in 1992, in which I wrote at least once daily, there is not a single mention of my brother. No word of my father. Though I remember that my brother fell very ill, late that year. On November 14, the day after a family wedding, my brother was admitted to Fairfield Infectious Diseases Hospital with pneumonia. I think the doctors believed, initially at least, there was a chance he had AIDS. Hence the location. In the photos from the wedding the day before, my brother's skin is parchment white. These are probably the last photos taken of him. We, my family, all stand, gathered in sunshine, outside a church at Black Rock.

I have this scrap of his handwriting, testimony from his work diary from his first day back after getting out of hospital.

I wonder, if my father or my brother walked into a room that I was in today, if I would recognise them.

I would recognise their handwriting.

Those words my brother uttered, *I'm never gonna die*, and the words that came afterwards about wanting to be buried on ancestor land, Ngurai-illum Wurrung Country, were not his last words, but they are the last words I remember.

To imagine these words, *I'm never gonna die*, is to engage the same form of magical thinking that I engaged with soon after, believing my father and brother to be

in trouble,

Not drowning.

Not dying.

Not dead?

What was my brother's last thought?

Did he think—

I am going to die

The instinctive drowning response dictates that a drowning person's body directs all possible resources to keeping the mouth above water, so I know there was little space for pondering death, but did he, did either of them, know they were approaching the end? There was time.

Did my brother tempt fate with his claims to immortality? This is the question I pondered in conversation with a police crisis counsellor two weeks later. There is no answer to this question.

As far as magical thinking goes, isn't it like a magic trick that a living person might slip beneath the border of an opaque surface and then not merely die, but *disappear?* Forever. As far as sleight of hand goes.

I wonder when the last time I truly saw my father was, before the last sight of him as a drowning man. I cast my mind back, wondering: was it his prediction of bad weather? That scene set in shades of yellow—the ute, sun-faded summer grasses, saturated with the intensity of colours before a storm. My father dressed in blue under one of the huge old ironbark trees, pointing at the sky.

Or is it the sight of him on the small platform beside the channel, upstream of the spillway? In this moment he is about to dive in, the sun is at his back, water to his front. Believing this to be a passing moment, without consequence.

And my brother? Is it the declaration of life everlasting, sitting in the remains of the ruined garden? In the back of the ute opposite me, benign wind on his face, his hand resting on the dog's black fur? Or finally, the moment after our father has entered the water and the dog has leapt in beneath the turbulent waters beyond the downward spill and churn? That fleeting moment of urgency, and agency?

If I can choose, then I choose my father about to dive into the water, and my brother claiming in his customary tongue-in-cheek way that he is never going to die. Both of them strong in their belief of so many good days ahead.

In Victorian times, mirrors and windows were covered after a death, so as not to reflect anything left shining. Everything was covered in black crepe. As though bandages for the dead. Or the still-living.

The duende, by contrast, won't appear if he can't see the possibility of death, if he doesn't know he can haunt death's house, if he's not certain to shake those branches we all carry, that do not bring, can never bring, consolation.[15]

What are you?

Where are your traces, now,
in the world?

We are storied fragments,
like drifting leaves,
but unlike rocks,
whose structure maintains.

The dead protect no one from anything. And the unimaginable is not impossible. Is as close as the interval after the next breath.

I think again of the green shoe chest in my mother's shed. The glimpsed objects: HSC windcheater but also small boxes that once held (whose?) coffee cups, filled with now-obsolete graphic-design paraphernalia. I wonder if I could piece together another version of my brother if I could only have access to these things, the things underneath them, that I have not seen. If I could gain entry—

Might I not hear your voice?[16]

After the 2011 earthquake and tsunami in Japan, a phone box (disconnected) to speak to the dead was installed in Otsuchi, one of the prefectures most devastated by the disaster. The phone box was installed by Itaru Sasaki at the bottom of his garden in an act of commemoration for his cousin. It came to be known as the "wind phone." Sasaki said he wanted his thoughts to be carried on the wind to the dead. Word spread and Sasaki allowed other mourners to share the phone to speak to their own loved ones.

For the living know that they will die, but the dead know nothing, and they have no more reward, for the memory of them is forgotten.[17]

In the dining room of the house we were living when my father and brother died, my father had installed an arrangement of photographs and painted portraits. All but one of the images were antique representations of ancestors in sepia tones. We called it the dead wall. The single image of a living person was a framed silver-gelatine photograph of my father, one of a series of portraits of him taken by my brother. In it, my father stares out, serious-eyed, bushy-bearded, wearing a formal white shirt. It would have been easy to have mistaken him then for a long-dead person from another era, among those other framed photographs. One of my mother's first acts upon returning to this house after my father and brother had been buried was to pull this framed photograph down from the dead wall.

Where are the police statements? Where is the coroner's report? Was there ever an autopsy report? My mother says she doesn't know. She can't remember.

Late on a Friday afternoon, in the mountain town where we live, my daughter points with dismay to the remains of a recently flattened king parrot on the road by a busy roundabout. *Yes, it's a pity*, I say and lead her away. Weeks later I walk across this road and notice the hollow bones transformed to a shape like a windmill or a flower, the outstretched wing pinned, flesh eroded; beautiful if you look away quickly enough.

I remember once, when I was a child, touching an electrical element behind an ancient round enamel light switch in a dank laundry outhouse. The resulting shock felt like someone had thumped me across the back with all their might. I looked behind me in shock and anger before realising what had occurred. The memory is etched sharply in my mind. I sometimes wonder if this is how sudden death feels as it comes upon you, as foremost an outrage.

For the first ten years after the accident, I was able to give an untroubled verbal account of what had happened. Early on, I became aware of the distancing employed, as though telling a story about strangers, or an anecdote recalled from a newspaper. I remember precisely how long it took for this to change: on the tenth anniversary of the accident I was at the Doulton Bar in St Kilda with friends, and when I went to tell some part of the old story one more time, I found I could no longer talk about it with ease. It took ten years to seem real.

I sometimes hear people retelling their experiences, in an untroubled way, of traumatic events that have happened. I recognise that quality of distance, and wonder how long it will take for it to sink in.

Though I say that I could talk easily about the drownings in the first ten years, this was not always the case. One Valentine's Day in the late 1990s, for instance, I helped a florist to prepare flowers. I was removing thorns from roses with a small metal implement. The drownings came up and, when prompted, I began to talk about it, to describe what had happened, but each time I began, I snapped another long rose stalk, until the florist hurriedly suggested a change of subject.

In 2004, my sister's memoir *Midnight Water* was published. On the day it was released, I went to a bookshop during my lunch hour and purchased a copy. I began reading on the tram on the way home that afternoon and didn't stop until I had finished. I remember the strangeness of reading someone else's portrayal of myself and everyone else in our family. More discomfiting for me than this was my sister's use of pseudonyms for everyone except herself, a choice she had made to preserve the privacy of family members, especially in the town where the accident had taken place. The name given to the "character" of "me" was Katy. It was unsettling to read about what happened to "Katy," but it reminds me in a way of how I used to tell the story of the accident, as something that had happened to other people.

At the book launch, my sister introduced me to her literary agent as Dani, "or, Katy."

I have a photo of my father, taken in the 1970s or early 1980s on what must have been a hunting trip. An old friend of his gave my mother some copies of it several years ago. My mother and I can't agree which one of the men in the photo is my father. I say he is the man in the centre, with his face obscured by the binoculars that he is peering through. This man has bullets slung on a bandolier that wraps around his waist, is criss-crossed over his chest, and slung around his neck. In his right hand, he holds a rifle. I assert that man is my father from the way he holds his body, his posture, and the performative nature of the costume and pose, the askew sense of humour that I recognise being on show. My mother insists that my father is the man on the left, pale-haired, face cast downwards, features rendered unclear as if the photograph has been under-developed. In this man's face and posture, I recognise nothing.

When John Keats died in 1821, a plaster cast was made of his smooth face—a death mask. Previously, Keats had also had his living face cast in plaster—a life mask. Both likenesses are hauntingly beautiful, and though the original death mask was lost, the mould was retained, and so versions of Keats's lovely face remain in collectors' hands. Casts were also made of his hand and his foot, but these were also lost ... if anything is ever really lost.

The death mask appears grainy, as though only ever past/passed, no possibility of present. As if watered, weathered by sea, as though ancient, timeless, as if encrusted with verdigris, as if lost a hundred, a thousand times, found and lost again. The mask is beautiful but is in a way so much worse than decay—like the body of tiny Rosalia Lombardo in the Capuchin Catacombs—it is so uncannily preserved, or *present,* that there is no sense of passing *away.*

I am unsettled by the absence of the cast of Keats's foot. I think of the way that only the head of the Tollund man was preserved, how his feet were left to rot, after all that time intact. I think of the absence of the Pompeii bodies, also cast in that white.

Here lies one whose name was writ in water.[18]

But his face is inscribed on harder surfaces.

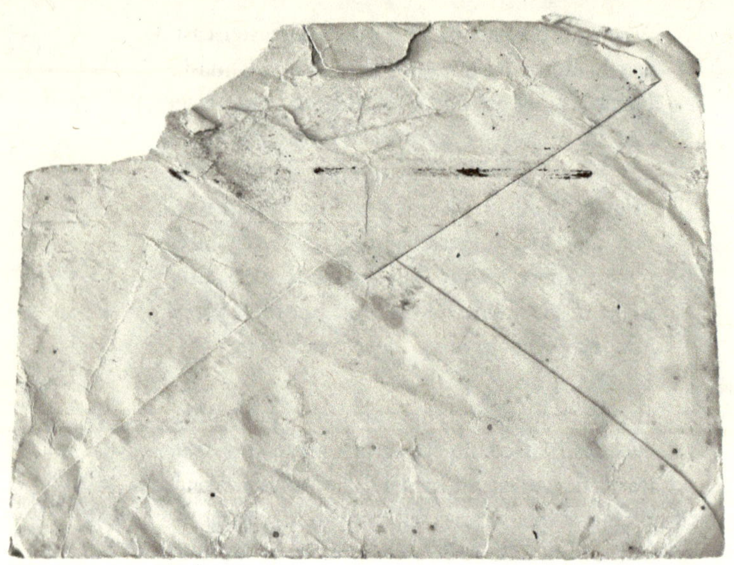

I imagine faces cast in plaster occupying those [not] spaces (air). I can imagine my father, his face wouldn't be too much changed from a life mask, if one existed (I can imagine him acquiescing to such a request), perhaps missing his dentures, so there would be a concave shadowing, small, not terrible, not terribly shocking. Like Keats's mouth, his mouth would be closed; his lips might turn downwards, as if resolute about endings. His eyes would be closed. The eyes are always closed on death masks, aren't they? No O-gapes rendered there, those voids.

It is a further distance, to try and imagine my brother's face so peacefully, pleasingly, poetically cast. It would limn a new visage, I know—

Not him anymore.

One of the most revered death masks in history, considered the most beautiful, is that of the woman they call *L'Inconnue de la Seine*, or the unknown woman of the Seine, who drowned late in the 18th century. Albert Camus referred to the death mask of her face as the *drowned Mona Lisa*. The face of *L'Inconnue de la Seine* was later used as the model for early versions of CPR mannequins (to breathe life back into).

During the last day of my grandfather's life, he had slipped into the deep sleep that often precedes death. Family members sat with him all day. There had never been any conversation about death and so, each time I had left him, there was no adequate farewell. When I left him this day, I leaned in close and pressed my forehead to his, which made him rouse slightly from his opaque slumber. I murmured to him that I loved him and said goodbye properly. That day is one of my most cherished memories. His face was as if already in the presence of death, passing into flux. One eye hung grotesquely open, though unseeing. A nurse covered it in a gauze patch to make it less confronting. There was a terrible hole behind his ear that seemed fathomless. But it was *his* face. *Him*. Beloved.

There are no death masks of my father's face or my brother's face, of course. Their bodies were not recorded in this antiquated, handcrafted way. It is remotely possible that forensic photographs were taken. When each was pulled from the water, perhaps, or on the autopsy slab. There might be a file in a storeroom, or on a hard drive somewhere. Would I want to view them if I could? My immediate, visceral reaction is still to recoil, to say no, but after this hesitation, I know that if there were pictures, I might eventually want to see them. That I might possibly steel myself, to be able to say—I will set eyes upon you, nothing about you could ever be (unbearable).

I would lay my eyes upon their images as though laying a hand upon a body, each body, perhaps a foot, a toe. A final act of tenderness, to say goodbye, to lay that idea of their damage to rest. To see them stilled, and still visible.

]and know this

]whatever you
]I shall love
] 19

The corpse, any corpse, can be read as a text. They are as Pompeii bodies. Nothing but space and remembrance.

In the week after the funeral, some of my brother's closest friends visited his Brunswick share house and gathered up his things. I think they took his clothes away, and then I think that can't be right, but I don't remember ever seeing them, those chambray shirts, the faded jeans and tan loafers, shorts and runners he wore to play netball. The white shirts, his uniform as a waiter in a small bistro in Abbotsford. The Tintin T-shirts he used to wear so often in the year before he died—we buried him in one of these.

It would have been too much to have seen such things at the time. If I saw such items now, I think that everything might come undone, even after all these years. These clothes seem spectral. Imagine them, unfilled clothes haunted by the shapes of a body's absence.

On the thirtieth anniversary of the drownings, my sister posts a photograph of her sitting on a rock on a beach, two weeks after the accident. In the photo, she is wearing my brother's beautifully tailored white shirt with narrow pleats on the front. In this image, my sister's face is crumpled and pale.

My mother seems ambivalent about allowing entry to the box in her shed filled with my brother's possessions. Perhaps for the same reason. It is still too much. For her, that would be a form of exhumation—as painful as exhumation—to unpack that box. Who packed it full of his things? It used to hold the family's shoes, many years ago. It did not come directly from his share house. Did it?

Who packed bulldog clips and angle rulers and a collection of erasers and other graphic-design paraphernalia into boxes that had previously held coffee cups? Whose coffee? It occurs to me that I don't even remember if my brother drank coffee. If he drank tea, like my father drank it, black, no sugar.

Was it the friends who packed up after his death? Or was it my mother, having once sorted through these possessions before putting them out of her sight for so many years? Who could not bear either to part with these them nor to look upon them?

There is another box, a little trunk made of shiny, decorative Mexican tin. This trunk belonged to my brother. It contains his good Derwent coloured pencils, and other things. His modest CD collection: INXS, Jackson Browne, Hothouse Flowers, and others. Once I pulled one of these CDs out of its cover and found a (his?) fingerprint on the reflective surface. I held my breath as though this fragment of possibility might disappear, and I placed the silver disc carefully back inside its cover.

This reverence for close-enough to a body.

I know,
a fingerprint
holds
so little trace.

Though, through DNA, so many stories can be held in such a trace, yet we cannot hold a fingerprint, or kiss it goodbye.

On what would have been my father's 75th birthday, packing up my mother's house as we prepare to vacate the ancestor land, Ngurai-illum Wurrung Country, my mother hands me a large striped plastic bag of objects and documents. It contains:

A plastic shopping bag with my brother's baby toy, a dilapidated stuffed cloth Mickey Mouse doll with silver tape around the broken neck semi-successfully holding the insides inside. An object I thought went into the grave with my brother.

My father's blue butcher's coat. A shade of almost-cerulean if I had to name the degree of blue. As I lift it out of the bag, it is almost as if birthing a baby, a caesarean emergence, via rupture, at least the remembered shape of someone that I loved.

My brother's woollen baby shawl, fringed, slightly stained.

An excerpt of my father's death certificate.

My brother's 1992 diary.[20] Also coloured blue. In the section featuring the following year at the back of the diary, my brother has signed his full name in the space for the day after his death on January 2, 1993. For the day after his body is found, he has sketched a series of interconnected boxes.

Their wallets. An old black one of my father's that I recall from my childhood, with a map of Australia embossed on an inside flap, and the wallets that both men were using at the time of their deaths. Inside are their drivers' licences, yellow-paper tram tickets, library cards, my brother's student card from Victoria University, video-shop membership cards, handwritten phone numbers, bank cards. All fleshed with the hollowness of ghosts.

A bundle of keys, its metallic smell absorbed into the skin of my hands after I have enclosed them in my palm, the possessive curl of my fingers granting entry to nothing.

A gauzy pink nightgown and negligee that my father bought my mother when she was nineteen.
My brother's twenty-first-key birthday card, cushioned satin, contained in a box, like a coffin.

A white-collared T-shirt in soft indigo-coloured fabric. It has the name of my father's butcher shop in large white letters across the left breast; it would have rested above the wounded heart.

The coroner's report for each man, both telling an inaccurate story about the dog jumping from the back of my father's ute and into the turbulent water beneath the spillway of the irrigation channel, of my brother leaping in to save the dog and then my father following to rescue him. Of both men perishing.

A plastic folder filled with sleeves containing my brother's references and academic records.

A love letter from my brother to his girlfriend, never sent.

There is a time, on the day of the accident, that I tie the end of the orange rope to a clump of grass. My cousin at the other end of it, in the water. My father and brother already submerged. I hear or see the car driving on the dirt track that leads from the Waranga Basin and stand in the middle of the track to flag them down with wild movements of my arms. The two men in the vehicle stop and jump out. I don't recall what I say to them, but they run to the bank of the channel and pull my cousin out of the water, then go to the nearby farmhouse to call for help.

It's a slow news week. During this time, news outlets and reporters from women's magazines and newspapers have been harassing us for interviews, with some of them flying in helicopters over my grandparents' property. The local police intervene to ask for privacy. There is some story of the local police making a helicopter landing and confiscating the camera footage from the news crew. This seems far-fetched now, but it is a story we hear that week. And everything about that time is surreal. The tantalising news angle is regarding me having witnessed the deaths, and the multiplicity of the family deaths. For days the story appears on front pages of newspapers. In the headlines, I am a "teen." "Teen sees father, brother, drown." "Teen's agony." At the time I wonder what the headline writer can possibly know of my pain. I wonder how they dare to try to spell out my devastation.

In the days between the recovery of brother's body and the funeral, a large national newspaper approaches us for an interview. They say if we don't grant it, they will attend the coming funeral and ask anyone in attendance for quotes. They later do a two-page spread for their Saturday edition. Its title is "Field of dreams," for the ancestor land, Ngurai-illum Wurrung Country, that my parents were building a mudbrick house on, that we left from to go to the channel. In the interview, I thank the men who stopped, who left without leaving their names, saying that we would like to meet them. The men, a pair of fishermen, come forward, and my cousin meets them and thanks them for saving his life. I wish I could have thanked them, too, for not leaving me as the only person walking out of there.

Always there is this sense of the proximity of my own death too.

Any of us could have died. All of us. Every single one of us, and I was first to the water's edge, but I stopped there.

There is a period over the spring where we are packing up my mother's house over a series of weekends, when another of the irrigation channels is almost emptied of water, though there has been a surplus of La Niña rains. You can see the small slate stones that line the channel. In this channel, the height or depth looks only slightly more than that of a standing man. My father and brother were both six feet tall, or thereabouts. Though they weren't standing.

In 1991, two years before the deaths of my father and brother, a "wet" mummy was accidentally discovered within a glacier in the Ötzal Alps, on the border of Austria and Italy. The mummy, later nicknamed Ötzi, was found to be the remains of a copper-age man, more than 5,000 years old. Ötzi, determined to be a murder victim from the flint arrow found embedded in his shoulder, had what was first counted as fifty-nine tattoos in groupings located at sixteen (meridian) points all over his body. The marks were composed of straight lines and intersections, made by rubbing charcoal into small incisions in the skin. It is believed that these markings form an early use of therapeutic healing tattoos, and that they had probably been inscribed to treat Ötzi's pain and ailments.

In 2012, the American artist Nicole Wilson undertook to emulate Ötzi's tattoos on her own skin. Wilson had the markings inscribed by a tattoo artist using her own blood as ink, via the same methods of small incisions that were used by Ötzi's tattooists. Wilson's tattoos were quickly absorbed back into her body, but the markings left behind dark heme scars that faded over time. Wilson recorded the process of the marks fading via a series of photographs. In 2016, after two further tattoos were discovered on Ötzi's body, Wilson recreated the tattoos on her own body a second time and again recorded the slow fade of the markings on her skin. Wilson terms the impulse of recreating the tattoos on her body as a *poetic action* that punctuates the connections between bodies and the gaps in our knowledge of the past.

In the days between the deaths of my father and brother and the funeral, one of my brother's workmates had three tiny letters tattooed onto his leg. The letters were an acronym for the three-word nickname he had for my brother. *GBG. Good Buddy G—.*

I am also, or this is also a tattooing of names and healing marks, and their bodies [also] are shapes on the page. They stop and start and stop, as though an animation, but there is nothing left there to assume fluidity; they are not bodies that continue to write themselves. They are inanimate.

In the penultimate chapter of her memoir *Midnight Water*, my sister writes a chapter called "The channel." In it, she reimagines the accident. To do so, she must combine what she had taken in of my account with both her imagining of what happened and a reordering, so that the senselessness might make sense to her and to readers. This reordering does not tally with my memory, but this is part of what writing does. Or is. In "The channel" the story of the drownings begins with the words *The day grows hotter. It is time for a swim.* But my sister shuffles time and event. She has the four of us and the dog swim where only the three of us had swum earlier in the day, when my brother, cousin and I alone had leapt from that other, upstream bridge by the willow trees. She has us return to the ancestor land, Ngurai-illum Wurrung Country, return to have the discussion about what our father and brother would like to have happen to them after they die. In this version, the fishermen that I flag down on the dirt track are already fixed in place, fishing from the bridge where the net will later hang. As though always watching—

"but otherwise they have the place to themselves."

In my sister's version, the dog is first into the water. She reimagines my account with such detail that I feel sure she is willing herself into that place, into where I am standing on the sharp yellow grass at the water's edge. I feel sure she is trying to insert herself into a space of impossibility and in so doing she is trying to prise open the blankness of her disbelief of a scene that will never seem true or real, but which is also hyper-real, painted full of colour, sound, event. As if, if she can somehow conjure herself as having been present, then she can change the outcome, or at least say goodbye with this one last sight. Also, so that she can place herself beside me at the water's edge.

Eavan Boland says such reimagining of other people's experiences are not meant to represent true stories, that they are *...more a rumour or a folk memory*, as though all such "memories" are constructed of longing. In "The channel," my sister has someone wrap me in their arms. She has someone drape a blanket around my shoulders. She steps into that space with love.

One week after my mother gave me the striped bag, we are preparing to leave for good in the coming days. My mother grants me entry to the green shoe chest. It is four days before we will leave this ancestor land, Ngurai-illum Wurrung Country. I throw much of the contents of the chest into garbage bags—my brother's old high-school and university assignments, old books, and magazines—but when I open the pages of business diaries from the late 1980s in the middle, my breath is taken away by the sight of many dense pages of my brother's handwriting. For two years, in 1986 and 1987, my brother had written accounts of his days. In the diaries after these years, he had given up this kind of writing, though he was still meticulous in documenting tasks that needed doing, and what had been achieved.

The diaries have the same precise reek of old paper as the old family documents my grandfather's cousin L— has gifted me, relating to the ancestors of the ancestor land, Ngurai-illum Wurrung Country.

Reading the two documented years, my brother is so vividly present that I laugh out loud, and sob and giggle. I am the shadow on the page, the one removed from these years. It is me who is absent, while he is more than whole, completely fleshed out. Alive. We meet once on the page, in the space of the night that is lost to me, the night of the car accident when I was twelve years old. On the day after that, he writes a dazed account of the incident, describing me as having been unconscious and covered in blood. The only detail he records of the hospital coincides with my one memory of that night, the moments when I am being wheeled in for a brain scan. He doesn't mention that within that interlude—maybe the reason the detail stuck in my mind among the rest of the amnesiac night—he is sobbing in our mother's arms.

Between these pages,
these two volumes,
my brother is found.

I cannot ask
for more

than this body,
composed of text.

Here is only a small archive, beginning with water's edge, with dives and leaps, and the act of staying still, of *efforts in vain*, and ending with cairns made of blue slate rocks, rumours of faint traces of smiles. Ending with nets, with underwater foliage, with immersion and catches. With what couldn't be seen or saved, and which can't be altered.

Except in these ways.

This is no act of prosopopoeia. There is only quiet. No epilogues but my own. My living hand, un-haunted in the act of writing. These are the limits of language, inexorable stillness, like a book that has ended and the author has disappeared, is lost.

Dead quiet.

To write elegies is to realise there is no end to the sentence. Their bodies are untranslatable.

We are powerless to stop the dead from disappearing. I live in the margins of grief and trauma. I am laid out there, prone, or else swimming beside these blank pages of absence. Body and presence. Or, I am the absence, and their bodies are interred in the margins of these pages, all pages, an erratum to my life. Preface, footnote and afterword to my days. These are my gatherings. My offerings for all the dead.

And for the girl I was before the rupture.

I studied the writing that these hundred-year-old letters contained. I transcribed them all. They were long separated from their envelopes by then. The envelopes were a scattered heap. It is a miracle they kept their shapes at all. Yet still, they are here, beautiful in their damaged states.

Even emptied,
they make sense.

We are setting out. Leaving this ancestor land, Ngurai-illum Wurrung Country, behind us now—

It's time to swim.

I am first to the water's edge.

Notes

1 Horner, Doug, "Bring up the Bodies," *The Guardian*, 2020.

2 Feigelman W, Jordan JR, Gorman BS. "How They Died, Time Since Loss, and Bereavement Outcomes," *Omega* (Westport).;58(4):251–73, 2008–2009.

3 García Lorca, Federico, "Theory and Play of the Duende."

4 Since the time of writing, Richard Flanagan has published his book *Question 7,* in which he does write in harrowing detail about this experience.

5 Caruso, J, *Decomposition Changes in Bodies Recovered from Water*, 2016.

6 Chapple. A & Ziebland. S, "Viewing the body after bereavement due to a traumatic death." 2010.

7 My mother's stepmother died in 2023. The ring was not returned.

8 "Drown agony," *The Herald Sun*, 1993.

9 "The Grauballe Man," *North*, 1975.

10 García Lorca, Federico, *Theory and Play of the Duende*, translated by A. S. Kline, 2007. Permission kindly granted by Adam Kline, *Poetry in Translation*.

11 Later, I have realised this phrase derives directly from my sister's imaginative recreation of the scene in her memoir *Midnight Water*, as if the real and the imagined accounts have intermingled.

12 Higher School Certificate.

13 My sister and I wrote in our father's obituary in the newspaper,"'Our own bush tucker man." He used to show us the white bodies of witchetty grubs beneath the bark of trees. He would pull them out and pop them into his mouth.

14 As narrated by our mother.

15 García Lorca, Federico, *Theory and Play of the Duende*, translated by A.S. Kline, *Poetry in Translation*.

16 Slessor, Kenneth, *"Five Bells," Kenneth Slessor: Selected Poems*, HarperCollins, 2014.

17 Ecclesiastes 9:5.

18 Part of epitaph on Keats's grave.

19 Carson, Anne, *If Not, Winter. Fragments of Sappho*, Vintage Books, 2002.

20 One of them. For unknown reasons, my brother had four diaries in the last year of his life, as if trying to fit as much in as possible, a kind of prescience.

Works Cited or Referenced

in order of appearance

Sarah Manguso, *The Guardians*, Granta Books, 2012.

Felicity Plunkett, "Becoming the Sea" from *A Kinder Sea*, UQP Poetry, 2020. Permission kindly granted by author.

"No title," *The Albury Banner and Wodonga Express*, 1906.

Michael Cunningham, *The Hours*, HarperCollins, 1998.

"Waranga Basin Waters," *The Riverine Herald*, 15 December 1908.

Marc Chagall, *The Creation of Man*, 1958.

Doug Horner, "Bring up the Bodies," *The Guardian*, 2020.

Gaylene (Indigo) Perry, *Midnight Water*, Picador, 2004. Permission kindly granted by author.

Kenneth Slessor, "Five Bells," *Kenneth Slessor: Selected Poems*, HarperCollins, 2014.

William Shakespeare, "Hamlet," *Shakespeare: The Complete Works*, Clarendon Press, 1988.

W. Feigelman, J. R. Jordan and B. S. Gorman, "How They Died, Time Since Loss, and Bereavement Outcomes," *Omega*, 2008.

Richard Flanagan, *Death of a River Guide*, McPhee Gribble, 1994.

Federico García Lorca, *Theory and Play of the Duende*, translated by A. S. Kline, *Poetry in Translation*, 2007. Permission kindly granted by Adam Kline.

"Drowned on His Birthday," *Adelaide Chronicle*, 22 February 1908.

Led Zeppelin, "Whole Lotta Love," 1969.

Mario Vittone, "Drowning Doesn't Look Like Drowning," 2013.

Francesco A. Pia, "The Instinctive Drowning Response," 1974.

Helen Garner, *This House of Grief: The Story of a Murder Trial*, Text Publishing, 2014.

Grant Perry, "Perry's Butcher's" sign, circa 1988.

Dragon, "Rain," 1984.

Gaylene (Indigo) Perry, "Crystals," 1993, first published in *Verandah* 8, 1993. Permission kindly granted by author.

"Drown Agony," *The Herald Sun,* 1993.

Jean-Jacques Beineix, *Betty Blue*, 1986.

Richard Lowenstein, *Dogs in Space*, 1986.

Howard Hawks, *His Girl Friday*, 1940.

Henry Koster, *Harvey*, 1940.

Joseph L. Mankiewicz, S*uddenly, Last Summe*r, 1959.

Sylvia Plath, "The Moon and the Yew Tree," written in Oct 1961, first published in *The New Yorker*, 1963.

"Double Fatality: Two Drowned," *The Daily Telegraph* Launceston, 1912.

Anne Carson, *Nox*, New Directions, 2010.

Kate Middleton, *Ephemeral Waters,* Giramondo, 2014.

Julia Kristeva, *Powers of Horror*, translated by Leon S Roudiez, Columbia University Press, 1982. Permission kindly granted by Columbia University Press.

Emily Bronte, *Wuthering Height*s, first published 1847.

Michelle Tom, *Ten Thousand Aftershocks*, HarperCollins, 2021.

"Man and Youth Drowned: Waranga Basin" *The Herald* Melbourne, 1928.

Dani Netherclift, "When Alive, My Brother Bore No Resemblance to Mermaids," first published in *Westerly* 67.1, 2022.

Michael Ondaatje, "Wells," *Handwriting*, Bloomsbury Press, 1998.

Behrouz Boochani, *No Friend But the Mountains*, Pan MacMillan, 2018.

Van Morrison, "Gloria," 1964.

Thomas Hardy, *Far from the Madding Crowd*, first published 1874.

"Drowned in Waranga Basin," *Shepparton Advertiser*, 1942.

Richard Flanagan, "Out of a Wild Sea," from *And What do you do, Mrs Gable? New and Collected* Essays, Penguin, 2011.

Jim Crace, *Being Dead,* Viking Press, 1999.

Anwen Crawford, *No Document*, Giramondo, 2021.

Georges Franju, *Le sang des* bêtes (*Blood of the Beasts)*, 1949.

J. Caruso, "Decomposition Changes in Bodies Recovered from Water," in *Academic Forensic Pathology*, 2016.

Gaylene (Indigo) Perry, excerpt from "The Sea-Blue Background," 2002. Permission kindly granted by author.

"Mother and Son Drowned," *The Sunday Times* (Sydney), 1912.

A. Chapple and S. Ziebland, "Viewing the Body After Bereavement Due to a Traumatic Death," *The BMJ*, 2010.

T. Ryback, "Evidence of Evil," *The New Yorker*, 1993.

Paul Celan, "Todesfugue," translated by Pierre Joris, *Memory Rose into Threshold Speech: The Collected Earlier Poetry*, Farrar, Straus & Giroux, 2020.

Caroline Sturdy Colls, "The Hidden Graves of the Holocaust," *Journal of Conflict Archaeology*, 2012.

"Five More Drowned at Weekend," *The Canberra Times* ,1993.

Helen Garner, "At the Morgue," *True Stories: Selected Nonfiction*, 2010.

Lia Purpura, "Autopsy Report," *On Looking*. Sarabande Books, 2011.

"The Drowning Case Near Echuca," *The Herald*, 1887.

Hippolyte Bayard, "Self-portrait as a Drowned Man," 1840.

Caravaggio, *The Seven Works of Mercy*, circa 1607.

Sarah Moss, *Cold Earth*, Allen and Unwin, 2009.

Corey Kilgannon, "Reopening Old Wounds: When 9/11 Remains are Identified, 20 years later," *New York Times*, 2021.

Wislawa Szymborska, "Photograph from September 11," translated by Clare Cavanagh, *Monologue of a Dog*, Houghton Mifflin Harcourt, 2006.

Brian Doyle, "Leap," 2015.

Sarah Senior, "What Bobby McIlvaine Left Behind," *The Atlantic*, 2021.

https://casetext.com/case/wtc-families-for-a-proper-burial-v-city-of-new-york.

Deborah Lutz, "The Dead Still Among Us: Victorian Secular Relics, Hair, Jewellery and Death Relics," *Victorian Literature and Culture*, Volume 39 (1), 2011.

Walter Benjamin, "The Storyteller," *Illuminations*, Penguin, 2015.

P. V. Glob, *The Bog People*, Faber, 1977.

Seamus Heaney, "The Grauballe Man," *North*, Faber and Faber, 1975. Permission kindly granted by Faber and Faber.

Federico García Lorca, *Theory and Play of the Duende* translated by A. S. Kline, *Poetry in Translation*, 2007. Permission kindly granted by Adam Kline.

J. Sime, "Exhumations: The Search for the Dead and the Resurgence of the Uncanny in Contemporary Spain," *Anthropology and Humanism*, 2013.

Sam Mendes, *1917*, 2019.

A. Rosenblatt, *Digging for the Disappeared: Forensic Science After Atrocity*, Stanford University Press, 2015.

Stacey Kish, "Why did the Atomic Bomb Dropped on Hiroshima Leave Shadows of People Etched on Sidewalks?" *Live Science*, 2021.

Will Higgins, "Poetry Inspired by Dead Bodies," *Indy Star*, 2014.

"Another Rural Tragedy", Bendigo Independent, 1912.

Ocean Vuong, *On Earth We're Briefly Gorgeous*, Penguin, 2019.

Audrey Magee, *The Colony*, Allen and Unwin, *2022*.

A. E. Stallings, "Refugee Poem" from *Like: Poems*, Farrar, Straus and Giroux, 2018.

Andrew Dominik Dir. *One More Time With Feeling*, 2016.

Anne Carson, *If Not, Winter: Fragments of Sappho*, Vintage Books, 2002.

Laura Imai Messina, "How Japan's Wind Phone Became a Bridge Between Life and Death," *Literary Hub*, 2021.

Ecclesiastes 9:5.

Eavan Boland, from the recording of "The Archive Project," Poetry Downtown Podcast, 2008.

Acknowledgements

The writing of this work was carried out in Australia on never-ceded Taungurung Country, and the writing within the book is often set on Ngurai-illum Wurrung Country. I acknowledge the traditional custodians of these lands, and pay my respects to Elders past, present and emerging.

Vessel came into the world as the creative artefact of my PhD, and I was lucky to have Briohny Doyle as my first supervisor, beginning the journey with me. Halfway through, David McCooey, who had helped me consolidate my first ideas about the form this work would take, became my principal supervisor. I am grateful for his gentle and kind mentorship, always bringing out the best in my words. And in the same vein and spirit,

I am grateful to Terri-ann White and Felicity Plunkett for their work on bringing *Vessel* to life in the first instance. And profound thanks to Leigh Nash, Andrew Faulkner, and Debby de Groot for believing in *Vessel*'s potential to go further into the wider world.

I'd like to acknowledge how invaluable the National Library's Trove database has been to me both in the writing of this book and generally. Speaking of libraries, thanks must also go to the librarians at Deakin University, who always go above and beyond.

To the #debutcrew24, many thanks for the support and friendship along the way.

Thanks to Simon, for your unflagging belief in me as a writer, and your enduring friendship.

To everyone in my family—mother, brothers, sister, and beyond—I thank you for your grace and love through difficult times, and for your forbearance in being, more than once, the subject of writing.

Thank you to Al, Perry, and Suzanne, none of this would be possible without your love, and without loving the three of you.

This book is dedicated to the memory of my father, Robert Perry (1947–1993) and to my brother, Grant Perry (1967–1993), and, finally, to my great grandmother, Colina Anderson nee Cameron (1891–1991), the addressee of the letters whose envelopes feature in *Vessel*.

Dani Netherclift is a writer and poet living on unceded Taungurung lands in the Victoria High Country, surrounded by mountains. She lives with her husband, son, and daughter, and recently completed a PhD in creative writing at Deakin University. Her area of research is the lyric essay and its intersections with white space, elegy, and the body. She has been published widely. *Vessel* is her first book.

Printed by Imprimerie Gauvin
Gatineau, Québec